This Incomplete One

This Incomplete One

WORDS OCCASIONED
BY THE
DEATH OF A YOUNG PERSON

Edited by

Michael D. Bush

WILLIAM B. EERDMANS PUBLISHING COMPANY

GRAND RAPIDS, MICHIGAN / CAMBRIDGE, U.K.

Wm. B. Eerdmans Publishing Co.
255 Jefferson Ave. S.E., Grand Rapids, Michigan 49503 /
P.O. Box 163, Cambridge CB3 9PU U.K.

Printed in the United States of America

11 10 09 08 07 06   7 6 5 4 3 2 1

Library of Congress Cataloging-in-Publication Data

This incomplete one: words occasioned by the death of a young person /
edited by Michael D. Bush.
        p.   cm.
ISBN-10 0-8028-2227-4 / ISBN-13 978-0-8028-2227-7 (pbk.: alk. paper)
1. Funeral sermons.   I. Bush, Michael D., pastor.
BV4275.T55 2006
252′.1 — dc22

                                                    2005032913

www.eerdmans.com

For Jo Hepburn,
in memory of Jonathan

CONTENTS

Foreword   ix
  NICHOLAS WOLTERSTORFF

Acknowledgments   xi

Editor's Introduction   xiii

Casey William Alley   3
  M. CRAIG BARNES

Matthias Barth   9
  KARL BARTH

Erik Hansen   21
  DAVID L. BARTLETT

Patrick Mills   27
  RONALD P. BYARS

What Can We Expect of God?   33
  JOHN CLAYPOOL

CONTENTS

Alex's Death   53
    WILLIAM SLOANE COFFIN JR.

Words of Faith, Hope, and Love   61
    STEPHEN T. DAVIS

When the Waters Are Deep   67
    J. HOWARD EDINGTON

True Saints, When Absent from the Body,
Are Present with the Lord   79
    JONATHAN EDWARDS

The Last Enemy   109
    LAURA MENDENHALL

Standing at the Grave   119
    JEFFREY J. NEWLIN

Anne Elizabeth Kuzee   131
    JACK ROEDA

Reaching Out   137
    FLEMING RUTLEDGE

Sermon at Nathanael's Grave   145
    FRIEDRICH SCHLEIERMACHER

Where the Children Can Dance   155
    PHILIP TURNER

Surprised by Death   161
    JAMES VAN THOLEN

FOREWORD

There is no purple prose in these sermons, preached in the most painful of circumstances, the death of a young person. Language has been cut to the bone. They are intensely moving. And authentically Christian.

All of them give full recognition to our worth as embodied persons. All acknowledge that we were created thus, and that God pronounced his creation good. None says that we are really just souls who do not really belong on earth.

All affirm the great worth of our love of our children. None says that we should not be attached to our children in such a way as to be cast into grief upon their death. All declare the legitimacy and worth of love and grief. None says that it's not really so bad — that we should get over it, put it behind us, get on with things.

None says that God is pleased with the untimely death of this person. All see the death of a young person as something gone awry in God's world. All affirm with Isaiah that in the messianic age, "No more shall there be an infant that lives but a few days, or an old person who does not live out a lifetime" (65:20).

All affirm the each-and-every note that pervades Scripture. God does not merely desire the flourishing of the human species. God desires the flourishing of each and every human being — desires that each shall flourish here on earth until full of years. When ninety-nine are in the corral, the shepherd goes out to look for the hundredth.

None of the sermons stops here, however. In not stopping here, they are also authentically Christian. All find in Scripture something more to be said to the grieving parents, siblings, relatives, and friends. In the something more that they find in Scripture, they are fascinatingly diverse.

There are, though, two recurrent themes. Amidst the grief over the brevity of this child's life, there is gratitude for his or her presence in our midst. The child was a gift. The grief does not smother the gratitude. And death, they all affirm, is not the end. We grieve, but not as those who have no hope. Yet none says that since death is not the end, we should not grieve. Though grief does not smother hope, neither does hope smother grief.

Michael Bush, the editor, could have found many sermons preached by Christian pastors at the funeral of a child that are not authentically Christian — sub-Christian sermons, pseudo-Christian, barely Christian. He has done a great service by culling out these authentically Christian, grief-laden hope-affirming sermons.

NICHOLAS WOLTERSTORFF

ACKNOWLEDGMENTS

Thanks are due first of all to several families and their pastors who have been willing that one of the most painful realities in their lives be shared for the benefit of others. Most of the sermons in the collection are published by permission of their authors. These include M. Craig Barnes, "Casey William Alley," David L. Bartlett, "Erik Hansen," Ronald P. Byars, "Patrick Mills," John Claypool, "What Can We Expect of God?," William Sloane Coffin Jr., "Alex's Death," Stephen T. Davis, "Words of Faith, Hope, and Love," J. Howard Edington, "When the Waters Are Deep," Laura Mendenhall, "The Last Enemy," Jeffrey J. Newlin, "Standing at the Grave," Jack Roeda, "Anne Elizabeth Kuzee," Fleming Rutledge, "Reaching Out," and Philip Turner, "Where the Children Can Dance."

Karl Barth's sermon, "Matthias Barth," is published by permission of Theologische Verlag Zurich, and was translated for this volume by Dr. Richard Burnett of Erskine Theological Seminary.

Jonathan Edwards's sermon, "True Saints, When Absent

from the Body, Are Present with the Lord," is published by permission of the Works of Jonathan Edwards Project at Yale University. The director of the Works Project, Kenneth P. Minkema, prepared this new abridgement and notes.

Friedrich Schleiermacher's "Sermon at Nathanael's Grave" is published by permission of the University of Chicago Press, and of the translator, Albert Blackwell.

James Van Tholen's sermon, "Surprised by Death," was published in *Christianity Today*, May 1999, and is reprinted here by permission.

EDITOR'S INTRODUCTION

The first task of an editor, I have read, is to tell readers what they have in their hands. Such telling in this instance can only be warning: You have pain in your hands. You also are holding onto hope, but never is this hope exuberant. It is quiet, while the pain is loud.

To the preacher who must address the word of God to a congregation gathered around a small or young absence, words feel stupid and clumsy, and yet something must be said. This is a collection of a few of the less clumsy things that have been said on such occasions. The truth is that to feel words to be weak is, in Christian faith, an incursion of doubt. (When young people die there are many of these.) In every moment, however desperate, we can say with the Gospel of John that the Word is with God and is God both in eternity and in flesh, living among us. It is not crucial to know what, precisely, this means. But it points to someone who was God living a human life, who died young and then showed that God thinks dying young, or dying old for that matter, is not the last word on life. It may not seem to be much, but in truth such a word is more than you might have dreamed. We shall have to trust God, as have these preachers, as must every preacher and hearer, for the word of God in their words.

The sermons presented here could be categorized and presented in several different ways. Three of the sermons (those by Karl Barth, Friedrich Schleiermacher, and Jonathan Edwards) have historical importance because they are by theologians we all recognize to mark high points in the history of Christianity. The Barth sermon, in particular, stands out in this regard, since it is published here for the first time in English. Five of the sermons are occasioned by the death of the preacher's own child. Ten of them were preached at funerals or memorial services. One is occasioned by the preacher's own impending death. In the end it has seemed best to present them simply in alphabetical order by the names of the preachers, in order to maintain a sense of the preciousness of every young person whose life and death we remember.

The collection is imperfect in some ways. Too many of the preachers are Presbyterian, too many are male, and all are white. In the end I am thankful for the diversity that is here rather than mournful for what is not.

The young people we remember here ranged in age into the thirties when they died. Most were infants and children. How can we not say, whatever it costs, that in some obscure sense they lived the full span of their days? Certainly it is so, if God is present, and good, and active. Yet saying this does not undo what we can only experience as the painful incompleteness of their lives. The image is Karl Barth's, who spoke of "the completion of even this incomplete one." This has come to seem an apt title.

The temptation to analyze and explain, to make comparisons, draw contrasts, and mark connections, besets me. For the most part, however, I have resisted. Each sermon is prefaced with a brief introduction to the preacher and the approach he or she has taken, and, often, some information about the deceased. Beyond this it seems best in this context to let the sermons and their preachers speak for themselves.

This Incomplete One

Casey William Alley

M. CRAIG BARNES

Craig Barnes's funeral sermon for Casey William Alley, a three-week-old baby boy, shows how much hope can be spoken in a short compass if words are chosen well and deployed aptly. The sermon is brief but is at the same time a luminous recommendation of the faith of the church in the powerful love and loving power of God.

Today Barnes is on the faculty of Pittsburgh Theological Seminary and is pastor of the Shadyside Presbyterian Church in Pittsburgh. This sermon comes from the period of his pastorate in Madison, Wisconsin.

Casey William Alley

ROMANS 8:38-39

For I am convinced that neither death, nor life, nor angels, nor rulers, nor things present, nor things to come, nor powers, nor height, nor depth, nor anything else in all creation, will be able to separate us from the love of God in Christ Jesus our Lord.

ROMANS 8:38-39

Our text today tells us, "Nothing can separate us from the love of God." Like all of God's promises, this one has to be believed to help us. Especially when we are looking at a little coffin.

This is not an easy day. No one will stand up today to talk about all the laughter and great experiences we had with Casey. There is no eulogy describing his long years of devoted commitment to family and service. No celebration of great achievements. That is because we are giving Casey back to God after only three short weeks.

Giving? No, maybe even that is saying too much. Today

5

we are mourning the loss of this precious little baby who was taken from us before we were ready to let him go.

It is amazing how quickly we all fell in love with this baby. We rooted for him in his struggle to live another day, and were in awe that so much courage and tenacity could fit into so small a body.

In such a short time, he left us all a little different. Casey taught us how to value the incredible gift of another day. His short, little, courageous life screams out to all of us never, ever to take the day for granted. We are all different for knowing this baby. Which means Casey was a grace from the love of God in our lives. And grace is one of those things from which we can never be separated. Not even by death. But you've got to choose to believe that.

On this day in which we are mourning the loss of the baby, let us not compound the tragedy by also losing our ability to believe. How many times now have we stood in church to say, "I believe in God the Father Almighty . . . the communion of saints . . . the resurrection of the body, and the life everlasting"? Why do we say these words Sunday after Sunday? To prepare us for days like today. For years and years we have gathered into this church to affirm our belief, because we knew the day would come when faith was the only thing that could get us through.

Well, now that day is here. And we will survive the grief, and the questions that do not have answers. We will survive by leaning into our faith. If you don't have enough yourself, then lean into the faith of the church. But don't dare try to grieve without believing the heavenly Father has received Casey into his eternal arms, or you will never survive the loss.

Not only does our decision to believe in the grace of God get us through death, it also allows us to give thanks for the three precious weeks we had with Casey. Again, this is a choice, and maybe one of the most heroic choices you can be asked to make. But it's the only way you're going to survive. If you choose to resent the loss, your heart will eventually turn dark and you will be unable to love anything in life. But if, in time, you get to the place of choosing to give thanks for the gifts Casey brought into our lives, you will discover that some of his childlike tenderness has been left behind in your own heart.

Give thanks for all the love that poured across his crib from an adoring mother, father, family, and friends. For doctors and nurses who threw their lives into giving Casey another day of life. Give thanks that God has always enjoyed incarnating his love for us in little babies. Give thanks that this eternal love, wrapped in so fragile a package, lives on.

So maybe this is a celebration of life after all. Maybe the thing we most want to say today is not that we are just so angry for losing Casey, but even more, that we are thankful for the life of this precious little boy. Even three short weeks with him was better than a life of never knowing him. Because in Casey William Alley, we received a glimpse of the love of God. And from God's love we are never separated.

Matthias Barth

KARL BARTH

Karl Barth was a twentieth-century theological teacher some have counted among the most gifted theologians in the history of the church. He was one of few theologians in Christian history who have spoken not only to their own age but to and for the church of the ages.

Barth preached this sermon in a memorial service for his son Robert Matthias on June 25, 1941, in Bubendorf, Switzerland. Four days earlier, Matthias had fallen to his death while climbing a mountain in the Swiss Alps. He was twenty years old.

This sermon is important because it shows clearly not only that Barth's personal faith held up in the searing experience of grief for his own child, but also that his theology held up as well. Many of the most distinctive and important themes of Barth's mature theology emerge again here from the crucible of his grief. An unresolved dialectic — in this case, of "now" and "then" — is here. The determination to hear the witness of Scripture speak in its own voice and to learn from it is here also. The focus on Jesus Christ as the key to understanding all reality is here. It is unmistakably Karl Barth's sermon.

In translating the sermon into English it was necessary for the logic of the sermon to preserve a literal representation of the idiomatic German rendering of 1 Corinthians 13:12, which speaks of seeing "through a glass in an enigmatic word," hardly good sense in English. The New Revised Standard Version has idiomatic English: "we see in a mirror, dimly." Barth, however, makes use of the idea of enigma and "enigmatic word" in the sermon, so that replacing it with idiomatic English would have made nonsense of parts of the sermon.

Barth was a Reformed pastor and theologian who spent most of his life around Basel, Switzerland, though he served a brief assistant pastorate in Geneva and taught in Germany for several years between the two world wars. At the time of this sermon he was teaching dogmatics at the University of Basel.

Matthias Barth

....

1 CORINTHIANS 13:12

*For now we see through a glass, in an enigmatic word; but
then face to face.*

1 CORINTHIANS 13:12

I chose these words because they were perhaps one of the
first Bible verses that made a curious impression on our
Matthias.[1] This verse is found beneath a picture of an old

---

1. Robert Matthias Barth, born on April 17, 1921, in the manse of Safenwil,
was the fourth child of the Barth family. During his first semester of theological studies he went on a mountain tour in the Berner Oberland. On Sunday,
June 21, 1941, at the Fründenhorn, a mountain in the massif of Blümlisalp, east
of Kandersteg in the valley of Kander, he fell. He died the following day in the
Frutigen hospital where his mother was able to see him for a brief moment
while he was still conscious. The funeral took place in Bubendorf (Baselland).
This is where Markus, Barth's oldest son, was a pastor. The sermon is available
in typewritten form — apparently done before the funeral. In addition to the
sermon there is a prayer and a biography of the deceased written by Barth and
read before the sermon. It also included an account of the accident in the
mountain. (Regarding the accident, see *National Zeitung*, Nr.284 of June 24,
1941, and Nr.285 of June 24, 1941, p. 9.)

theologian that Matthias saw daily in our home.[2] During our time in Bonn when he was still a rather young student, I discovered by chance that he had copied this verse down in Latin, and it appeared that he had been contemplating it: *Videmus nunc per speculum in aenigmate, tunc autem facie ad faciem.*

And now we have come from the grave where we laid his poor broken body to its final rest. We have just now heard a few brief indications of what his short life was about.

We are here in order to set what has happened, and our Matthias and we ourselves who would so much love to call his name again, in the comforting and liberating light of God's Word. And for this situation I do not know a better verse than this: *"For now we see through a glass, in an enigmatic word; but then face to face."*

Because God's grace has come to help us in our misery through our Lord and Savior Jesus Christ, thus it is so: wherever and however we live our life with all its hopes, weaknesses, and secrets, both are true, both — whether we know and understand it or not — deeply and indissolubly united with each other: the Now! but also the Then! They are not separate from each other but entirely together: The Now where we see very well and understand everything, yet we do not know at all what everything is like in reality. And the Then, where we will see everything clearly and where all will be glorious. The Now: a mirror in which everything is turned upside down; an enigmatic word, which certainly

---

2. The picture Barth is referring to is a copper engraving with the portrait of August Neander (1789-1850), with a facsimile of the Scripture verse in Neander's handwriting and his signature.

gives us an answer but at the same time remains the most difficult question. And the Then: where we will not only be known by God, but we ourselves will know him no less fully than he knows us.

It is by the grace of our Lord Jesus Christ that the Now and the Then are together in such a way that no power in heaven or on earth can separate them again. For it is he alone who in his bitter death on the cross and in his glorious resurrection has bound the Now and the Then together so that even now there is no mirror or enigmatic word that does not have standing behind it the clarity of that seeing face to face. And every single beaming ray of the future glory of God will be nothing but a particular turning and adjusting of the reflection before which we now stand, a particular resolving of the riddle we are now trying to figure out.

This is the grace of our Lord Jesus Christ, that we follow him and may stand with him at the border where the Now and the Then touch each other, that we at this border may believe, love, and hope. It is at this border where light falls into darkness, where life always rejoices in the face of death, where we are great sinners yet righteous, where we are taken captive yet free, where we see no way out yet we have hope, where we have doubts yet we are certain, where we weep yet we are glad.

In our thoughts about our Matthias we do not want to put ourselves in any other place than precisely at this border. He has now crossed over it, and we are still here. But we are not far from each other if we put ourselves at this border. In Jesus Christ there is no distance between Now and Then, between here and there, however profoundly they are separated. Our Matthias — just as he really was — is in Jesus Christ, yet very differently than the way he used to live with us and we with him. He is the same, yet he has become completely different. Because Jesus Christ has taught us about both, about life and death, death and life, we may now therefore remember our Matthias and thus speak about him.

In a special way it was true of him that he saw not only divine things but also human things, the things of this world, "through a mirror in an enigmatic word." Everything was immersed in the sphere of his imagination. Everything was related to his own creative longing, the fulfillment of which he then playfully thought he could find in certain historic figures and circumstances and in sometimes solemn, often ironic, presentations of their inner and outward character. It was this very longing that already in his childhood made him occasionally, for the sake of some impossible venture, forget space and time. It also led him past the reasonable demands of school even after he eventually learned outwardly to meet those demands. It concerned him in all the joys and disappointments he experienced with his peers. It also surely led him precisely to the mountains. Everything was always a little different in reality than it was in his thoughts and intentions. In spite of his quick mind he never stopped dreaming childhood dreams. He seemed to experiment with the outer world and its tasks, with people, with his own strengths and possibilities.

And it is quite possible that he approached theology in the way one used to approach this mother of all disciplines in times of old: without having to give an exact account of the particular subject matter with respect to a beginning which could be followed by entirely different consequences. At any rate, he approached it with some personal idea regarding his own aspirations and desires, the feasibility of which would have had to have proven itself, first of all, in theology and the pastorate. He would have fit, in any case, in this world better at the beginning of the nineteenth century rather than in our time, for its contradictions, its excitements, and its demands struck him as somehow strange, if not hostile.

But for him the Then is already effectively Now, beyond the mirror and the enigmatic word. He now sees that which he obviously meant and wanted to see in our Now: face to face, knowing God and all things in such a way as God himself has known him throughout eternity. Being "in Jesus' arms and lap"[3] he now truly knows it better than his father and his brothers. Could it be that he, like Joseph, already here dreamed more about the true reality of life [Genesis 37:6ff.] than he knew? Could it be that he was right to a large extent that we considered him a "pure fool"?[4] We do not know and we do not have to know. But we may know this, if

3. These words come from the third verse of N.L. Zinzendorf's hymn, "Die Christen gehn von Ort zu Ort durch mannigfaltgen Jammer" (1731), GERS (1891) 326; GERS (1952) 250:

> Wir freun uns in Gelassenheit
> der großen Offenbarung;
> indessen bleibt das Pilgerkleid
> in heiliger Verwahrung.
> Wie ist das Glück so groß
> in Jesu Arm und Schoß!
> Die Liebe führ uns gleiche Bahn,
> so tief hinab, so hoch hinan!

4. A "pure fool" (*reiner Tor*) is a "person who is a stranger to the evil of this world" (Brockhous and Wahrig, *Deutsches Wörterbuch*, vol. 6 [Stuttgart: Weisbaden, 1984], p. 253). It is in this sense that Richard Wagner uses this word in the first act of *Parsifal*.

we stand with Jesus Christ at this border where the Now and the Then touch, and if we think about our Matthias from here, we may know that although here these things were for him only vague recollections, there pure glory shall fill his eyes. We still see them so clearly before us, his expectant — yet somehow always unfulfilled — gaze, and then all of a sudden, beaming eyes. These eyes shall Then see; they see Now, face to face. And we want to rejoice with him. We are delighted for him that he may there see so very differently.

Our Matthias was certainly quite often a mirror and an enigmatic word in his conduct and behavior: not so transparent in what he really wanted, he did not easily adjust to or accept situations that were initially uncomfortable for him. The same was true with respect to plans that were not initially clear to him. He was not easy to deal with, for example, when he entered into certain armistice treaties regarding school.

When he was still very young, Matthias once played the role of a "wanderer" in a performance at our home. With his father's big cane and hat, all he had to do was walk across the stage and then disappear again. We who knew him well, but certainly also others, have seen him come from a distance only to disappear again into the distance as such a wanderer.

I still see him before me as a nine-year-old when he joined us on a mountain trail which was much beyond his strength, light-footed, hardly touching the ground, not in the least concerned with us or any possible dangers, jumping from rock to rock like a little billy goat. Even where he felt at home he always seemed somehow away, somewhere else. I do not think anyone knew him well enough to say he fully understood him.

In an amazingly frank moment of self-recognition, he just recently said to me, "You know, I simply do not have any life-experience at all!" He indeed had no life-experience in spite of the rich education he had at his young age. And this is probably the reason it was so difficult for us and others to understand him, that he was such a mirror and enigmatic word. We expected that through military service he might perhaps feel more at home in the human world and would become more intelligible and approachable,[5] but we also asked ourselves whether this somewhat coercive course might possibly have an entirely different effect upon him. That expectation as well as this concern have now been invalidated. He was granted to conclude his Now in the same way he had begun it; he was granted to be and to remain the wanderer he had always been. But precisely because this Now has been closed behind him because of the Then which his life has suddenly entered we no longer need to be concerned about all the disconcerting things of his life.

In order to truly understand our Matthias and his mysterious and very short wandering way, to truly understand the beginning and the end of his journey that so often surprised us, we have only to recognize that Lord who was crucified and risen for him as well.

We no longer see him and the astonishing things about him, because he walked straight into the beaming ray of the resurrection of his Lord and ours and vanished from our

---

5. Matthias Barth was to report for duty in early July, 1941, and receive seventeen weeks of basic training in the Swiss army.

eyes. But we do not see this beaming ray and do not see in it who and what our Matthias was: a man for whom the Son of God gave himself so that he, the inexperienced one, would not perish but have everlasting life [John 3:16]. This is true and was "then" meant for him. If we see and remember this, if we seek him there, even now we have understood him as much as we need to. We cannot then be surprised that even now, in spite of everything, we loved him so much from the beginning and to the end just as he was. Thus it can be nothing other but that we still love him in our memories and always will.

And now there is his sudden earthly end: once again truly a mirror, an enigmatic word of an especially painful and terrifying kind. He came to take his final summer journey through Switzerland up into the mountains from which he did not return alive. The twenty-second of June then came and presented us with another great riddle,[6] and finally on that night, Matthias quietly left us. The rest of us then had to deal with the bitter hours and days of an inner farewell, with lingering questions: Did we not owe him much more while he was still with us? And what strong desire to take his hand just one more time, which he liked so much, and to speak a good word to him just once more. But what are we, what can we do, what do we know, of what use are all our questions, our contemplations, and desires in the face of the great, inexorable mystery of death?

6. In the early morning hours of June 22, 1941, Hitler ordered more than three million soldiers to march into Russia ("Operation Barbarossa"). The official declaration of war, which was joined by Italy the very same day, followed one and a half hours later. This was the beginning of the campaign in Russia and the expansion of World War II into eastern Europe.

Again and again I had to think during these days about the words David said in Second Samuel 12:23 about his dead child: "Can I bring him back again? I will go to him but he will not return to me." And more than ever it surprised me that with these words David wanted to justify why he would no longer fast and cry. Indeed, if there were no resurrection of the dead revealed through Jesus Christ as the first fruits of those who have fallen asleep [1 Corinthians 15:20], David would then have to be called a strange, heartless father. If the dark Now would not be so close to the bright Then and inseparably connected with it, how then could David call this suffering for which there was no cure, the very reason he would no longer be sad? But Christ *has indeed* been raised from the dead, the first fruit of those who have fallen asleep. The mystery of Good Friday — the terror and pain of which the things we go through cannot even be compared — now has been followed by the resolution of Easter day. Jesus now lives, reigns, and is victorious.

The Then has come so close to the Now so that this Now of death is no longer a special realm of which we have to be afraid, or which we have to regard with questions and mourning, with fasting and tears. We see that death has power, terrifying and painful power. But we believe and we know that it does not have a deadly sting [1 Corinthians 15:55]. And even more: we believe and we know that death itself — after Jesus Christ suffered it in order to enter into his glory [Luke 24:26] — is merely, for those for whom Christ has suffered it, the path and service to the very same glory.

David therefore was right. Precisely where we must give up everything as lost, hidden beneath the sighing and tears which we are allowed to have, the appropriate thing for us is the full jubilation of those who even now may taste the life that waits beyond each grave.

A deep helplessness and defenselessness was perhaps something of our Matthias's innermost being. How could he have escaped the strong one who now, as in a storm, swept away his life that was so far from completion? But even now we believe and know that there is One who long since took this strong one captive, who long since took away his power to kill, who long since has forced him into his own service. This we shall see when we see him face to face. But the Then is very close to the Now. Therefore, in all our sorrow today, we cannot merely mourn.

Even if we cannot rejoice ourselves, we still hear an entirely different voice rejoice even over the evil spot at the Fründenhorn where everything happened, also over the grave from which we have just come. This voice speaks about the completion of even this incomplete one, about his completion as God's servant brought about through death. It speaks about peace and joy and life to the fullest [John 10:10]. What else can we do as we hear this voice but thank our God — even if in tears — that he fulfilled his good will and purpose in the life and the death of our Matthias? And with us, too! "I am," Jesus says to us, "the resurrection and the life" [John 11:25].

Erik Hansen

DAVID L. BARTLETT

Depression deep enough to lead to suicide is a darkness that threatens to overcome the light. In his memorial service sermon for Erik Hansen, a bright young seminary student, David L. Bartlett speaks with frankness not only of Jon's intelligence, love, courage, and faith, but also of his "pact with the enemy." By speaking of the anger as well as the grief of those left behind when Jon took his own life, Bartlett handles with sensitivity and grace one important task for the preacher in such situations: he identifies the situation, including its emotional dimensions, to which the gospel must speak if it is to be heard.

This sermon was preached July 21, 1986, at the American Baptist Seminary of the West, where Erik Hansen was a student. At the time, Bartlett was pastor of the Lakeshore Baptist Church in Oakland, California. Today he is Distinguished Professor of New Testament at Columbia Theological Seminary in Decatur, Georgia. "Erik Hansen" is a pseudonym.

Erik Hansen

For I am persuaded that neither death nor life, nor angels nor principalities nor powers, nor things present nor things to come, nor height nor depth, nor any other created thing, shall be able to separate us from the love of God which is in Christ Jesus our Lord.

ROMANS 8:38-39

What can we affirm in the face of such a tragic loss? The gift of life. The reality of death. Our Christian hope.

We affirm the gift of life. When death has done its worst, it cannot take away from the goodness we knew and loved in Erik.

There was his intellect, of course. The superior work he did as a scientist. The connections he was trying to make between that world and the world of theology. The sharp, often unanswerable questions. The seeking.

There was his love of people. Even in the most difficult struggles, he cared for those who struggled with him. His trust and confidence in Terri were very deep, and his sorrow for her sorrow. The decision they made together to think more about her future, her dreams — that was a gift of strong and lasting love. And his friends: We heard their names — friends from his youth, from Pullman, from here. He did win love and give love.

There was Erik's courage. It took courage to move from the world of science he knew well to the world of theology, with its odd jargon, its dense books, its apparent distance from what can be seen and touched. It took courage to move away from the beloved world of Pullman to the iffier worlds of American Baptist Seminary of the West and Lakeshore Church.

"I'm not much of a hero," Erik said to me once. But I told him that every day he fought off the darkness that was always threatening, every day he did that he won a heroic battle. And the fact that for a time, at least, the darkness won, does not diminish one iota Erik's extraordinary courage.

And we remember the gift of Erik's faith. It was a faith caught up in the Gospel prayer: "I believe; help thou my unbelief." It was a longing for God so intense that the days of God's absence seemed like a personal affront, a hope for God so deep that Erik risked more than most of us will ever dare.

With all the loss, all the pain — how much we loved him, how much we liked him — we affirm the gift.

We also acknowledge the reality of death. The apostle Paul, who wrote the words we have heard from Romans, knew nothing of "natural death" and not much of death with dignity. For him death was the enemy, always an unwelcome intruder, interrupting, violating life.

Today we know what Paul meant. Death had no right to lay claim over Erik, and when we are honest we think that Erik had no right to make a pact with the enemy.

We feel guilt, that we should somehow have been stronger, found the right words, forged the weapon that would have allowed Erik to fight off death.

We feel loss. All that bright promise taken from us so soon, so soon.

But we affirm our Christian hope. "I am persuaded that neither death nor life, . . . nor things present nor things to come, nor height nor depth, nor any other created thing, shall be able to separate us from the love of God which is in Christ Jesus our Lord."

Death *is* the enemy. Death and depression and despair and awesome anxiety — all death's minions are the enemy.

But Christ is the victor. That is the faith by which we live, and the faith to which we die, and the faith in which we entrust our beloved dead to the care of God.

"I am persuaded that neither height nor depth will be able to separate us from the love of God in Christ Jesus our Lord."

Not the depth of sorrow which Erik felt and which, for a time, overcame him. That cannot separate him from the love of God.

Not the depth of loss we feel that Erik is taken from us. That cannot separate us from the love of God.

Not the depth of our anger. That cannot separate us from the love of God.

Not the depth of our guilt. That cannot separate us from the love of God.

Neither height, nor depth, nor any other created thing will be able to separate us from the love of God in Christ Jesus our Lord.

"I am persuaded that neither life nor death will be able to separate us from the love of God."

I am persuaded that God's love for Erik is stronger than death's power. I am persuaded that the death of Jesus Christ in terrible abandonment and the resurrection of Jesus Christ in light and love are not just ancient tradition but present hope — for us, for Erik, for all those we love.

I am persuaded that neither death nor life — the saddest death, the most fragile life — neither death nor life will be able to separate us from the love of God in Christ Jesus our Lord.

So often sitting talking to Erik, I felt as though I was trying to grab hold of his deep, fundamental, loving goodness and keep it fast against every encroaching enemy. I think that's what we were all doing. Holding on to that dear life against death's sneakiness and power.

My faith is this: that what we could not do, our God has done in Jesus Christ. That God has now held fast the deep, astonishing goodness of his dear child. And keeps him safe. Forever.

To God, Creator, Son, and Spirit, be thanks and praise. Amen.

Patrick Mills

RONALD P. BYARS

Patrick Mills's mother once said to another bereaved mother, whose son had been hit by a car, "Mine is a different kind of tragedy." Patrick's death has the terrible facet of having been brought on by his own choice, though it was not suicide. Patrick died at a party in his fifteenth year of life, unconscious from the effects of substances he had introduced into his body.

It is hard to imagine how a pastor could deal with the realities and emotions of Patrick's death with more grace and perceptiveness than did Ronald P. Byars. His choice of a biblical text is perfect. King David has also lost a son, Absalom, as a result of the child's own terrible choice. The fact that the child chose this way in defiance of his parents does not make the parents' grief less. If anything, it makes it greater. "If only I had died instead of you!"

At the time of this sermon, Byars was pastor of Second Presbyterian Church in Lexington, Kentucky. Today he is Professor Emeritus of Preaching and Worship at Union Theological Seminary in Virginia.

Patrick Mills

2 SAMUEL 18:32-33

The king said to the Cushite, "Is it well with the young man Absalom?" The Cushite answered, "May the enemies of my lord the king, and all who rise up to do you harm, be like that young man." The king was deeply moved, and went up to the chamber over the gate, and wept; and as he went, he said, "O my son Absalom, my son, my son Absalom! Would I had died instead of you, O Absalom, my son, my son!"

2 SAMUEL 18:32-33

It's a fundamental act of faith to bring children into the world. As fearless as we may have been as young adults, as soon as we become parents we all at once become aware of how dangerous the world is. We watch the child, lest she fall off the changing table while we're reaching for a diaper. We warn the child to stay out of the street, teach him to cross at the green lights. We tell her not to stick a fork into the toaster. As the child grows older, he or she ventures farther and farther from home, less and less subject to the scrutiny of parents. We find ourselves lying awake at night for the sound of the car in the driveway. In the newspapers we read terrible stories, and visualize our child as the central figure in every conceivable tragedy.

We know that it irritates our child when we offer our various warnings: don't stay out too late; don't drink and drive; remember you have that paper due tomorrow. We know these warnings are meaningless, utterly futile; that they have no result except to make the child angry at us. But we so desperately want to guard the child from danger. And so we offer our parting words simply because we need to say them, as though they were some kind of charm: "Be careful!"

In rational moments, of course, we know full well that there are forces in the world, forces in our children, forces in ourselves, from which we're absolutely helpless to protect them. Our urgent advice, our prayers, our sleeplessness cannot, in the end, shield them from harm.

The same goes for friends. We may see our friend going under, but we're powerless to hold her up. We want the power of our friendship to be enough, but when it isn't enough, there's nothing left but to feel sad or angry. Sad or angry because there are limitations on our power to help someone who doesn't think he or she needs to be helped.

Most of us, growing up, are lucky. We do foolish things, take crazy risks, and the odds are in our favor. We escape tragedy, and live long enough to get our acts together, and grow up, and worry about our own children. But not all.

Patrick was bright; he could be charming; he could be a loyal friend. He loved sports. A friend says that he wrote poetry. He was acutely sensitive to injustices. He was generous. He saw things from an original point of view, and many of his friends loved that quality in him. But Patrick was also chased by some demon. He'd been running, running for years. He was running away from something, and probably not even Patrick knew exactly what it was. Certainly none of those close to him knew. He could silence his personal demon with drugs; chase the demon away for awhile with alcohol. But the demon kept coming back; and Patrick kept on running.

In some times and places, young people have run away because they have a dream of somewhere they'd like to be. They run away and join the circus; run away and see the world; run away to pursue some ambition stifled at home; run away to have the opportunity to live out some dream. It's dangerous, but exhilarating, to be running toward something. There's life in that kind of running, health and vitality when we run toward something. But it's not clear whether Patrick had glimpsed something he might be running toward.

Patrick had received all the usual warnings about drugs. He didn't lack information. He knew the dangers of alcohol. But when you're running away from something, when the demons are at your heels, those warnings mean nothing. When he ran, Patrick became his own worst enemy.

In the Old Testament book of Second Samuel, the story is told of King David's son, Absalom. Absalom got into all kinds of trouble, and caused his family endless grief. Finally, he became overtly rebellious against his father. His father, King David, desperately wanted that no harm should come to his son, even though Absalom had shown less than zero respect. But harm did come to the young man. And when

David heard that his son was dead, he wept, and cried out, "O my son Absalom, my son, my son Absalom! Would that I had died instead of you, O Absalom, my son, my son!"

This is the cry that comes from our hearts for all our children. For the ones who make it, and for those who don't. For the ones who run toward some dream, and for those who know only to run away. For the ones who find a place in society, and for those whose dress and demeanor and speech and actions are calculated to keep mainstream society at a distance. This is the cry for all our children; and it's God's cry for each and every one of us: "O my son Absalom, my son, my son Absalom! Would that I had died instead of you, O Absalom, my son, my son!"

What Can We Expect of God?

JOHN CLAYPOOL

John Claypool's sermon "Life Is a Gift," which he preached soon after his daughter's death, is well known and has frequently been anthologized. The following sermon, which has not been anthologized before, dates from a time nearly two decades after her death.

Here Claypool speaks of the important question, "How can we handle the promises of God responsibly?" There are some situations in which it is responsible to expect a miracle. There are occasions when it is responsible to anticipate a solution in which human skill cooperates with the wisdom of God. And there are places in life when responsibility is expecting only that God will sustain us. Claypool's experience of Laura Lue's illness and death at the age of ten was, for him, one of the latter occasions.

The late John Claypool was for many years an Episcopal priest in Birmingham, Alabama. Previously, he had been a Baptist pastor in Louisville, Kentucky, where Laura Lue died.

What Can We Expect of God?

ISAIAH 40:27-31

[The Lord] gives power to the weak,
And to those who have no might He increases strength.
Even the youths shall faint and be weary,
And the young men shall utterly fall,
But those who wait upon the Lord
Shall renew their strength:
They shall rise up with wings as eagles,
They shall run and not grow weary,
They shall walk and not faint.

ISAIAH 40:29-31

C. S. Lewis did not marry until he was fifty-six years old. From all reports, the four years he shared with Joy Davidman were years of unusual and profound bliss. She had cancer when they first met each other. She had cancer when they married. And though most of the time they were together she was in remission, the disease did reappear. She had a prolonged period of suffering, and then she passed away.

35

In the days that followed her death, Lewis kept a very careful journal of his experiences, and wrote them down where he expected only his own eyes to see them. Shortly before his own death, which incidentally was the same day John Kennedy was assassinated, he was persuaded to take these journal entries and to publish them in a little book. It came out first under a pseudonym, N. W. Clerk. It was entitled *A Grief Observed.* If you ever have had a chance to experience that volume you will know that Lewis begins on about as shrill a note of disappointment as I have ever encountered.

You see, he had expected his Christian faith — for which he had been an exponent for many decades — to offer him a certain kind of consolation. And yet when he found himself in the valley of the shadow of grief, lo and behold, none of that materialized. Lewis reacted like anybody who feels they have been sold a bill of goods would. He has all the marks of a disillusioned person. And in those early pages, he makes no bones about it: he is disappointed in what God did for him in this very, very searing experience of grief.

If C. S. Lewis was anything, he was a profound and tenacious thinker, and therefore he did not stop with his initial impressions as he made his way into the valley. He probably knew from his profound readings that disillusionment is often the child of illusion. Perhaps he sensed that his extreme reactions at first had more to do with the expectations that he had constructed ahead of time than with what had occurred. And so, as the book unfolds, we see him going back and looking with a new sense at what actually had taken place, over against what he had expected ahead of time.

And, lo and behold, it turns out that God's other name here, as almost everywhere, was Surprise. That is, the transcendent One had not acted in a certain moment the way a finite creature had expected him to act. And therefore, as the book finally comes to a conclusion, there is a much different tone. It is as if Lewis has finally come to terms with the, "My ways are not as your ways" which God continually says to us. And so, at the end, he seems to be at a much greater place of acceptance.

I remember reading that book years ago and putting it down with a kind of shiver, because I said to myself, "How can we handle the promises of God responsibly? How can we keep people from being disappointed, in addition to everything else they are experiencing, by the way we talk to folk about what they can expect of the Holy One in history?" Anybody who knows anything about biblical revelation knows that it is filled with promises about what God will do for our kind of creature. "God is our refuge and our strength," says the Psalmist, "a very present help in time of trouble." "My God shall supply all your needs according to his riches in Glory," says the Apostle.

Or consider the words of Isaiah that I read tonight about "waiting upon the Lord." If we are willing to be accessible to God's strength, our strength will be renewed. We will rise up with wings like eagles, run and not be weary, walk and not faint. All of these are very specific promises about how the energies that pertain to the divine One become real to those of us who live in this kind of world.

The question I found myself asking was, how can we handle these promises in ways that don't set people up for disappointment? How can we, on the one hand, be faithful to what is promised, and, at the same time, do it in such a way that folk like Lewis, when they get to hard and difficult places, don't find themselves burdened with disappointment?

And so I began to look at the whole range of biblical material. I began to try to look at the patterns of how the divine interacts with the human. Tonight I would like to share with you what it seems to me is a comprehensive answer to the question, What can folk like us honestly expect of God in the daily workings of life in this world? If those promises mean that the divine somehow comes and becomes a part of our human life, what exactly can we expect of God? How does the transcendent One enter the stream of history and make contact with the likes of us?

Well, it seems to me that there is not one answer to that question, but three answers. There are three distinct patterns, it seems to me, in Holy Scripture that describe this mysterious interaction of the One who is above with life here in history.

For example, one of the ways that the energies of God enter into history and impinge upon the lives of human beings is intervention from beyond. Energies not of this realm suddenly become active in history, and people find the very circumstances in which their lives are housed to be dramatically altered.

A biblical illustration of this kind of intervention would be that passage in Mark's Gospel where Jesus is walking along and from a distance he hears a cry. It turns out to be from the lips of a man who is suffering from leprosy, a disease that was a terrible malady in the first century. It caused your skin and your strength to gradually waste away. It was so contagious that people who had it were isolated from everyone else. It was really one of the tragic, tragic dead-end conditions of that day. And a leper suffering from this kind of isolation calls out to Jesus as he is making his way, "Jesus, son of David, have mercy on me, a leper. You can heal me if you will."

And the story is that Jesus turns in the direction of this absolutely isolated and pitiful person and says, in effect, I do want to heal you. I do have the power. Be cleansed of your leprosy. And in an instant this man, according to the record, looks down, and the flesh is being reconstituted on his hands. Suddenly there is wholeness where once there had been sickness. Energies from some realm beyond the purely historical seemed to break in and alter the condition of that particular man.

I don't know what kind of presuppositions you bring to this very, very mysterious word, "miraculous." I don't know whether that word means something you close your mind to. I have no idea how each of us in this room feels about this business of miracle — energies breaking in from beyond and changing tangible circumstances.

I myself have been helped greatly by something that St. Augustine wrote many centuries ago. He said that what we humans call miracle has more to do with timing than anything else. He defines a miracle as God choosing to do quickly what God usually does at a more deliberate pace. And then he suggests that what happened on the plain that day, when Jesus was faced with a great multitude and he multiplied the loaves and fishes into far more than they had in the beginning, was God doing quickly what he usually does in a much slower time frame. He says that loaves and fishes are always being multiplied. Every time the wheat seed is put into the ground, and is carefully nurtured, and sprouts up and brings to bear the fruit of the wheat, and the wheat is harvested, and somebody takes it and makes it into bread, loaves are always being multiplied. But they are being multiplied at the slow, slow pace of nature. Or every time the fish swim upstream and spawn millions of eggs, they, too, are being multiplied. What God did there on the plain, for God's own reasons, was simply to do quickly what God is always doing at a more deliberate pace.

Now what that suggests to me is that in a real sense everything is miraculous. That anything exists, that anything has been called out of nothingness into being — that is the towering miracle. Whether the Mystery does it quickly or does it slowly is not as astonishing as the fact that anything exists at all. Therefore, my sense is that we would do well not to close our minds too quickly to the possibility of the surprising, to the transcendent One doing things in a different way than the way he usually does them. To be open to the miraculous is simply to be true to the data of history. It means not concluding, on the basis of certain assumptions, that things cannot happen, when in fact we finite creatures have no sense of what is possible in so vast a realm of mystery.

So it seems to me that there are times, both in biblical history and in our own history, when something we cannot account for occurs, and the plates of the earth shift under our feet, and for causes we can never identify circumstances get changed. God does something in a way God has never done it before. One of the things we can expect of God is that kind of in-breaking from beyond.

Now, having said that, let me say something else about this category of the miraculous:

This is the help from God we instinctively want first when we find ourselves in a difficult place. Every time we are faced with a situation that is beyond our power, every time we find ourselves with our backs to the wall, at the end of our rope, the first thing we want to do is to cry out to the transcendent One and ask that that One break in and change these circumstances and miraculously get us out of whatever it is we have gotten into. And sometimes, I believe, God chooses to do that.

Every one of us, no matter how old or how young, has at some time or another cried out and asked that God do something for us, just as that leper was crying out to Jesus.

And notice that Jesus himself, at the height of his maturity, close to the end of his own life, goes into the Garden of Gethsemane and looks at a set of circumstances that are very repulsive, and he does the same thing to the Father that the leper had done to him. "If it be possible, O God, let this cup pass from me."

Nobody in this room should feel guilty if, when you are really up against it, you lift your eyes to heaven and hope against hope that somehow energies from that realm will break into your realm and do something about your difficulty. It's the first instinct all of us have in a tight place.

But although there are times that that prayer is answered — although there are times, I believe, that there is this mysterious in-breaking — to think that this is the only way that God does his work in history is, I'm afraid, to set ourselves up for the kind of disillusionment that you see so often among believing people.

I know folk who strongly believe in the miraculous. And yet, they label the miraculous as the only category worthy of having the name "divine" attached to it. Unless there is a miraculous solution, they tend to think there is no action of God in history. And here is where I think dealing with the promises of God responsibly becomes very important. You see, I honestly believe that there are times that God does break in from beyond and change our circumstances, but that's not the only way the Bible suggests that the grace to help in time of trouble becomes active historically.

In fact, I would say there are two other forms of God's doing something in the midst of history that are just as valid as the in-breaking that we call miraculous.

The second way is what I call the pattern of collaboration. If there are times when, for God's own purposes, he breaks in and does something for us, there are other times when God comes to where we are and offers to do something *with* us. I am suggesting now that when the divine energies inspire us to be creative and ingenious, invite us to do something toward the solution of our problems, the collaborative form of God's coming is just as valid as the miraculous.

The biblical analogy for this would be that whole series of stories in the Old Testament about how God delivered the children of Israel from Egypt. They had come to Egypt at a time when the Pharaoh was very favorable to Hebrew folk. But then one and another administration came, and the Hebrews were made a slave people. And yet there was one in their midst named Moses who was raised up out of most unusual circumstances and is known historically as the "great liberator," the one who delivered the Hebrew people from the hand of the Pharaoh. It is a very long and involved story.

As you may remember, Moses was actually born of Hebrew parents but was adopted by the Pharaoh's daughter, and so at a very early age got the advantages of royal education. He could have forgotten all about the folk who were his native connection with history. There are always two kinds of people, the people who are interested in making the world a better place for everybody, and the people who are simply willing to make a better place for themselves in the world as it is. Thanks be to God that Moses was the former kind, the kind who could not forget the plight of his people, even though he himself had been delivered from it. And so as a young man with fire in his eyes, wanting to be a zealous reformer, he resorted to violence. He killed an Egyptian overlord.

I suppose Moses thought he would start a revolution that would lead to the setting free of the people. But it wasn't time for that kind of interaction. The Hebrews did not know Moses, or they were not ready in their own development, and therefore as a result of Moses having tried to cut the Gordian knot with violence, he was forced to flee for his life into the Midian desert. And there, for forty years, he seemed to waste away while the slavery continued.

And yet the truth was that he was being prepared for a vocation that would one day become his. He learned like the back of his hand — the way only a shepherd could learn — that sandy terrain across which he would eventually have to lead the people to freedom. God is often preparing us for things of which we have not the slightest inkling. And so it was, after those forty years when it seemed to him that everything was going nowhere, that a bush began to burn. He was attracted to it. God spoke to him out of this bush and said, "I want you to go and collaborate with me in setting my people free."

Moses said, "I'll be glad for you to do it, but I don't want to get involved with that Egyptian hierarchy anymore. Let's face it, I went to prep school with those guys. I know them. And I know they are not willing to let go this good deal they've got with the slaves."

God continued to say, "I want you to collaborate with me."

You see, Moses had wanted the children of Israel set free, and now God was saying, "If this is going to come about, you are going to have to become involved. This is not something I am going to do *for* the Hebrew people. It is something I have to do *with* them."

Let me pause and say that when most of us hear God say, "I want you to be a participant in the solution of your problems," we become very infantile. We back off. We would prefer a miracle. We would prefer for God to break in and do it all rather than to have to enter the very difficult process ourselves. We want the solution of God doing something *for* us, when in fact, the real agenda often is God doing something *with* us. And my sense from reading the Bible is that this is the form in which the grace to help in time of trouble most often comes into our lives.

There are certain problems you and I face that simply cannot be solved for us, problems that demand our participation. We talk so much about wanting to have a better and cleaner environment. That's not something that we just sit down in the chair and ask God to give us. That is a solution in which we must be costingly and courageously involved. We pray for peace, and well we should. But we also need to do what we can to work for peace and to bring down the levels of hostility. The point I'm trying to make is that many of the problems for which we very much need divine help are going to be solved when we yoke ourselves to the energies of God. Instead of asking God to do everything for us, while we stay babies, we begin to see that the invitation was the same that was given to Moses: "I want to set my people free, but you, Moses, are going to have to go down and confront the Pharaoh. You are going to have to go down and be a participant in calling the people to the courage to reach for their own freedom. You are going to have to use what you have learned about the Sinai Peninsula to lead these people across the desert waste." In other words, the collaborative way of God entering history is just as valid as the way of intervention and of miracle.

But I would suggest there is yet a third pattern of the divine entering history. Sometimes, for God's own purposes, he breaks in from beyond and does something for us. At other times, for God's own purposes, he comes alongside us and offers to do something with us. But there are some times, my friends, that the help that God offers us in history is simply the power to endure what cannot be changed, to allow the change to take place within us and our attitude, rather than in the outward circumstances that we face.

The biblical analogy for this is that passage where St. Paul reveals his own inner life, where he talks about the "thorn in the flesh" that he had struggled with for years. Nobody knows exactly what it was. It was some physical impediment that got in the way of his ministry. Some people think it was a continual attack of malaria, a disease that was common around the Mediterranean basin. Other people think it was his struggle with his own sexual impulses. I myself think the most likely possibility is that after his encounter on the Damascus road, Paul always had problems with his eyes. That is, the blinding light may have done something lasting to those eyes that he had in his head. In the Book of Galatians he says, "I have written this in my own hand; you can see how big the letters are." In another place he says, "You Galatians were so empathetic to me, you would have taken out your very eyes and given them to me." So it could be that it was a problem with his vision. But whatever it was, it was something that really bothered him, something that he had prayed to God could be somehow taken away. He had begged for miracle. He probably had consulted with the best doctors there were in that time. He had done everything he could about this daily difficult situation that he faced.

And one night it came to him as clearly as if the voice were speaking from heaven: "Paul, the thorn in the flesh is not going to be removed. But listen: My grace will be sufficient for you to bear it. I'm not going to change the circumstances. I'm not going to join with you in altering them. I'm going to give you the strength to stay in the midst of the unchangeable, and to learn in that situation to change your own attitudes and to grow on the inside rather than to change on the outside."

I don't know about some of you, but there have been times in my life when this offer of God's help simply to enable me to endure was the most relevant and the most powerful thing that ever happened. It is not as dramatic as having some miraculous cure. It is not as energetic and satisfying as some collaborative solution. But to be given the strength to endure what you cannot change, to stay in the midst of something that is as hard as a thorn in the flesh, and not to blow up in anger or to give down into despair — that, too, is one of the ways that God enters into our history.

Back in 1970 when I was living in Louisville, Kentucky, my second child, a little daughter, ended an eighteen-month fight with leukemia on one snowy Saturday afternoon in her own home. The battle with that disease was lost, and at ten years of age she made her way into the great land of the Mystery. Her illness had been an extremely difficult and painful time for everybody in our family. We were all exhausted physically, emotionally, spiritually.

About six weeks after she died, I was down visiting in Methodist Hospital in Louisville, and I ran into a Jewish rabbi who was a good friend of mine. We had not seen each other since my daughter had died, and he paused to tell me how sorry he was that this had happened. And then he caught me off guard by saying, "I want to ask you something — honest, man to man. Did God do anything for any of you in the midst of all that circumstance?"

I had not expected that question, and we were too close friends for me to give some kind of glib public relations answer. Here was a man from another religious tradition, a man whom I knew to be honest and truth-loving, looking me dead in the eye, and wanting to know out of a deep profound question, "Is there anything we can attribute to the divine that took place in this awful experience through which you have just come?"

I did not attempt to answer him quickly. I began to think. And I realized quickly that God had not performed the miracle of healing that I had so prayed for, and that lots of other people had prayed for. Laura Lue had not experienced that healing that the leper had experienced. I also realized that despite tremendously extensive medical collaboration, we had not been able to find the answer to this disease that was eating away at her body. The day she was diagnosed I asked her hematologist in my shocked condition, "Exactly what are we up against? How long are you talking about?"

He said, "I can't be specific, but I will tell you that the statistic for her age with this kind of leukemia is eighteen months from diagnosis to death."

She lived exactly ten days longer than the eighteen months. We used every medical strategy we knew to use, and none of it was helpful. There was no collaborative solution to her problem.

So God didn't miraculously break in. And there was no collaboration.

But then it began to dawn on me, quietly, that God had, in fact, done something for all of us in the midst of that struggle. That little ten-year-old girl became incredibly courageous beyond anything that anybody could account for. It was amazing. Even yet, I think back on the way she was able to handle some very, very difficult situations. Her brother was ten years old when the diagnosis was made, twelve when she died. I saw him emerge as a responsible person in incredible ways because of this thing that was happening to our family.

I could remember those times when I thought to my soul that I could not stand it for another minute. There was one day when they were trying to give her an injection. They could not find a working vein. They punched and punched and she cried in her agony and I thought to my soul, "I don't think I can stand it for another second." But the amazing thing is that somehow in the midst of the unspeakable, there was something that kept me from blowing up in anger or giving down in despair. I managed to stay there with her and for her, as did the whole family.

And so, I was finally able to look my rabbi friend in the eye and say, "Yes, I've got to be honest with you: God did give us something. He gave us the power to endure what we could not change. He gave us the power to stay with something, and instead of it defeating us and turning us bitter, somehow we were sustained by a strength that was not our own."

And I said, "I've got to admit to you that now I sense that I'm becoming something different because of having been given the gift of endurance. I must confess to you that life is more precious to me today than it was before this episode. I must confess to you that I had taken life for granted pretty much until Laura Lue got sick. Life had been very, very good to me. I had never been significantly crossed by tragedy. And therefore there was a tendency in me to simply up and take for granted this incredible gift of aliveness. But I'll never do that again. Having sensed how powerless I was to hold on to her life, having sensed that I could do so little for someone I loved so much, has made me that much more anxious to take every day as the gift that it is, and not to take for granted the people that I touch and I love, but to look on them as a kind of windfall, a kind of grace, and a kind of gift. I know with assurance that I have become a different person because I had to endure something I wasn't given the grace for changing."

And he and I talked for a long time about how the divine gift of endurance, which seems so undramatic, may, in fact, be one of the most potent and powerful ways that the grace to help in time of trouble enters into history.

What I'm suggesting tonight is that if you will open your faith to all three of these forms, if you will realize that at times what we can expect of God is the in-breaking of energies beyond ourselves to miraculously change circumstances; and that at other times, the energies come, inspiring us to join with God in finding a joint solution; and that sometimes, the only form grace takes is the power simply to hang in there and not give up — even that is a grace to help in time of trouble — if you will realize this, you will not be disappointed.

And as I thought down this road the words of Isaiah which I read for you tonight took on a new meaning. Listen again against the backdrop of these forms of divine grace to what the prophet says: "They that wait upon the Lord shall renew their strength." There really will be help in the midst of our troubles. And how does that help come, O Isaiah?

There are occasions when we will be given the strength to "rise up with wings as eagles." This is the intervention from beyond that lifts us out of circumstances, changes what we are up against. Sometimes we will rise up with wings like eagles.

At other times we will "run and not grow weary." This is the collaborative way of joining with God in the solving of our problems.

At other times, all we're given by the grace of God is the power to walk and not faint, the power simply to stay with the unalterable and not to blow up in anger or let down in despair, but just simply to move inch by inch. And, my friends, I suggest to you that this last form of God's grace, the least dramatic, may in fact be the most powerful of all.

Somebody has said that Isaiah has the sequence wrong,

that first we walk, then we run, and then we soar with eagles. But those people have never been where I have been.
They've never been in a hospital room with a little girl crying for all her heart's worth and realized that there is no occasion to soar, and no room to run. In those places, the
grace to walk and not faint is the very best gift in the world.

My contention tonight is that if you will let all three of
these become your vision, you will not be disappointed. In
the worst of times, that mystery beyond all understanding
will become a part of your life. If you will give God the freedom to do miracles when it's God's reason to do miracles
and not demand that that be the only solution; if you'll be
sensitive when he calls you into the fray to use your
strengths; and if you're humble enough to simply settle for
the strength to walk and not faint, I believe I can say, without fear of contradiction, you will not be disappointed.

"God is our refuge and our strength, a very present help
in time of trouble." Bet your life on it. Amen.

Alex's Death

WILLIAM SLOANE COFFIN JR.

If there is a classic in this group of sermons, surely it is William Sloane Coffin's "Alex's Death." He mounted the pulpit less than two weeks after his son drove his car into Boston Harbor, and preached this sermon.

It is always remarkable when a preacher deals in the pulpit with the death of his or her own child. Such preachers have a claim on our attention simply because they have been tested in a fire the rest of us have not known. A faith that is enduring that test, and has enough vigor in it to support the act of preaching anyway, is a faith that knows the reality of what is preached. Like too many others, Coffin knows.

When he preached this sermon Coffin was pastor of the Riverside Church in New York City. He is now retired and living in Vermont.

Alex's Death

PSALM 34:1-9; ROMANS 8:38-39

I will bless the Lord at all times;
his praise shall continually be in my mouth.
My soul makes its boast in the Lord;
let the afflicted hear and be glad.

PSALM 34:1-2

For I am sure that neither death, nor life, nor angels, nor prin-
cipalities, nor things present, nor things to come, nor powers,
nor height, nor depth, nor anything else in all creation, will be
able to separate us from the love of God in Christ Jesus our
Lord.

ROMANS 8:38-39

As almost all of you know, a week ago last Monday night, driving in a terrible storm, my son Alexander — who to his friends was a real day-brightener, and to his family, "fair as a star when only one is shining in the sky"[1] — my twenty-four-year-old Alexander, who enjoyed beating his old man at every game and in every race, beat his father to the grave.

Among the healing flood of letters that followed his death was one carrying this wonderful quote from the end of Hemingway's *A Farewell to Arms*: "The world breaks everyone, then some become strong at the broken places." My own broken heart is mending, and largely thanks to so many of you, my dear parishioners; for if in the last week I have relearned one lesson, it is that love not only begets love, it transmits strength.

Because so many of you have cared so deeply and because obviously I've been able to think of little else, I want this morning to talk of Alex's death, I hope in a way helpful to all.

When a person dies, there are many things that can be said, and there is at least one thing that should never be said. The night after Alex died I was sitting in the living room of my sister's house outside of Boston, when the front door opened and in came a nice-looking middle-aged woman, carrying about eighteen quiches. When she saw me she shook her head, then headed for the kitchen, saying sadly over her shoulder, "I just don't understand the will of God." Instantly I was up and in pursuit, swarming all over her. "I'll say you don't, lady!" I said. (I knew the anger would do me good, and the instruction to her was long overdue.) I continued, "Do you think it was the will of God that Alex never fixed that lousy windshield wiper of his, that he was proba-

---

1. This line comes from William Wordsworth's "She Dwelt among the Untrodden Ways."

bly driving too fast in such a storm, that he probably had had a couple of 'frosties' too many? Do you think it is God's will that there are no streetlights along that stretch of road, and no guardrail separating the road and Boston Harbor?"

For some reason, nothing so infuriates me as the incapacity of seemingly intelligent people to get it through their heads that God doesn't go around this world with his finger on triggers, his fist around knives, his hands on steering wheels. God is dead set against all unnatural deaths. And Christ spent an inordinate amount of time delivering people from paralysis, insanity, leprosy, and muteness. Which is not to say that there are no nature-caused deaths that are untimely and slow and pain-ridden (I can think of many right here in this parish in the five years I've been here), and which for that reason raise unanswerable questions, and even the specter of a Cosmic Sadist — yes, even an Eternal Vivisector. But violent deaths, such as the one Alex died — to understand those is a piece of cake. As his younger brother put it simply, standing at the head of the casket at the Boston funeral, "You blew it, buddy. You blew it." The one thing that should never be said when someone dies is, "It is the will of God." Never do we know enough to say that. My own consolation lies in knowing that it was *not* the will of God that Alex die; that when the waves closed over the sinking car, God's heart was the first of all our hearts to break.

I mentioned the healing flood of letters. Some of the very best, and easily the worst, came from fellow reverends, a few of whom proved they knew their Bibles better than the human condition. I know all the "right" biblical passages, including, "Blessed are those who mourn," and my faith is no house of cards; these passages are true, I know.

But the point is this: While the words of the Bible are true, grief renders them unreal. The reality of grief is the absence of God — "My God, my God, why hast thou forsaken me?" The reality of grief is the solitude of pain, the feeling that your heart's in pieces, your mind's a blank, that, in the words of Lord Byron, "there is no joy the world can give like that it takes away."

That's why immediately after such a tragedy people must come to your rescue, people who only want to hold your hand, not to quote anybody or even say anything, people who simply bring food and flowers — the basics of beauty and life — people who sign letters simply, "Your broken-hearted sister." In other words, in my intense grief I felt some of my fellow reverends — not many, and none of you, thank God — were using comforting words of Scripture for self-protection, to pretty up a situation whose bleakness they simply couldn't face. But like God herself, Scripture is not around for anyone's protection, just for everyone's unending support.

And that's what hundreds of you understood so beautifully. You gave me what God gives all of us — minimum protection, maximum support. I swear to you, I wouldn't be standing here were I not upheld.

After the death of his wife, C. S. Lewis wrote, "They say, 'the coward dies many times'; so does the beloved. Didn't the eagle find a fresh liver to tear in Prometheus every time it dined?"

When parents die, as did my mother last month, they take with them a large portion of the past. But when children die, they take away the future as well. That is what makes the valley of the shadow of death seem so incredibly dark and unending. In a prideful way it would be easier to walk the valley alone, nobly, head high, instead of — as we must — marching as the latest recruit in the world's army of the bereaved.

Still there is much by way of consolation. Because there are no rankling unanswered questions, and because Alex and I simply adored each other, the wound for me is deep, but clean. I know how lucky I am! I also know that this day-brightener of a son wouldn't wish to be held close by grief (nor, for that matter, would any but the meanest of our beloved departed), and that, interestingly enough, when I mourn Alex least I see him best.

Another consolation, of course, will be the learning — which had better be good, given the price. But it's a fact: few of us are naturally profound; we have to be forced down. So while trite, Robert Browning Hamilton's lines are true:

> I walked a mile with Pleasure,
>   She chattered all the way;
> But left me none the wiser
>   For all she had to say.

> I walked a mile with Sorrow
>   And ne'er a word said she;
> But oh, the things I learned from her
>   When sorrow walked with me.

Or, in Emily Dickinson's verse,

> By a departing light
> we see acuter quite

Than by a wick that stays.
There's something in the flight
That clarifies the sight
And decks the rays.

And of course I know, even when pain is deep, that God is good. "My God, my God, why hast thou forsaken me?" Yes, but at least, "My God, my God"; and the psalm only begins that way, it doesn't end that way. As the grief that once seemed unbearable begins to turn now to bearable sorrow, the truths in the "right" biblical passages are beginning, once again, to take hold: "Cast thy burden upon the Lord and He shall strengthen thee"; "Weeping may endure for a night, but joy cometh in the morning"; "Lord, by thy favor thou hast made my mountain to stand strong"; "for thou hast delivered my soul from death, mine eyes from tears, and my feet from falling." "In this world ye shall have tribulation, but be of good cheer; I have overcome the world." "The light shines in the darkness, and the darkness has not overcome it."

And finally I know that when Alex beat me to the grave, the finish line was not Boston Harbor in the middle of the night. If a week ago last Monday a lamp went out, it was because, for him at least, the Dawn had come.

So I shall — so let us all — seek consolation in that love which never dies, and find peace in the dazzling grace that always is.

Words of Faith, Hope, and Love

STEPHEN T. DAVIS

Susan Angell died on Easter morning, 1970, in an automobile accident. She was twenty-one years old. Her father, James W. Angell, described his experience with her death in a book, *Oh, Susan!* where Stephen Davis's sermon was first published.[1]

Stephen T. Davis is professor of philosophy of religion at Claremont McKenna College in Claremont, California. For this collection, Professor Davis has made minor corrections and emendations to the sermon as it first appeared.

---

1. James W. Angell, *Oh, Susan! Looking Forward with Hope after the Death of a Child*, revised ed. (Pasadena, Calif.: Hope Publishing House, 1990).

Words of Faith, Hope, and Love

1 CORINTHIANS 13

At present we only see the baffling reflections in a mirror, but then it will be face to face; at present I am learning bit by bit, but then I shall understand, as all along I have myself been understood. Thus "faith and hope and love last on, these three," but the greatest of all is love.

1 CORINTHIANS 13:12-13

Do you remember Catherine, the girl in Hemingway's *A Farewell to Arms*? On her deathbed, she says to her lover, Lieutenant Henry, "Don't worry, darling. I'm not a bit afraid. It's just a dirty trick." Christians cannot agree with this, for they believe that God is a God of love. But if they are honest they must admit that there are events that they cannot explain.

"In this life," Paul says, "we have three great lasting qualities — faith, hope, and love. But the greatest of them is love."

Faith at its deepest level is trust. To trust in God is to base

63

your life on the premise that whatever happens, you are in God's hands, and that these hands are loving hands. Faith is trusting in God despite the inexplicable; to have faith is to trust God anyway, despite the tragedies. It is to trust that whatever happens, there is a reason for it in the depths of God's love.

Hope at its deepest level is confidence. To hope in God is likewise to have confidence that whatever happens, you are in God's hands, and that these hands are loving hands. Some religions press hope to the point of denying tragedy. Christianity does not. The Christian faith is not a talisman to ward off trouble; it is not a rabbit's foot to bring good fortune; it is not a way of becoming thick-skinned to protect us from being hurt. Christianity admits that the tragedies of life are real and that they really hurt. But the Christian hope is that in the end even the tragedies will be explained and that the victims are safely in God's hands. To believe that God is a God of love is to hope for nothing less.

Love at its deepest level is God's love for us, not ours for God or for each other. To be a Christian is to believe that love conquers all, and that the God of love is always by your side. The psalmist said, "Even though I walk through the valley of the shadow of death I fear no evil, for thou art with me" (Psalm 23:4). To believe in God's love is to believe that whatever happens, you are not alone — you are in God's hands and these hands are loving hands. We sometimes think we are apart from God, untouched by his love; but even when we imagine we are far from him, even when we deny God, even when we hurt very deeply and inconsolably, even when there is something we cannot explain — even in those moments we are upheld by God's love.

Christ's death on the cross was also a stark tragedy. He was an innocent man, a great religious teacher in the prime of life, a force for good; and he was tortured horribly and executed on the flimsiest of excuses. There were some who loved him standing by at the cross. No doubt they felt as confused, as cut off, as deeply hurt as we do today. But they were not alone. No matter how much they suffered, God was beside them, and his love sustained them — the very love that later explained the tragedy by means of the resurrection. Christians believe that God's love carries us through life, undergirding us all the way. And they also believe that his love for us culminates in our resurrection. Not even death can separate us from God's love, for death is not the end. We can live eternally in God's presence.

Susan Angell knew the power of love. She was that rare person, an individual beautiful both inside and out. She loved music. She loved the out-of-doors. She loved people. She loved Pomona College, where she flowered as a person. Her four years there were years of fulfillment and happiness. She loved Kierkegaard and Tillich and other theologians. In short, she loved life. I am convinced that in the final analysis these loves were really ways of loving God. For she knew that the only thing that really matters and endures in life is love, and God is love.

Once, when entering Jerusalem, Jesus implied that even inanimate objects could praise God. The Pharisees wanted him to rebuke the people for welcoming him, to which he replied, "I tell you, if these were silent, the very stones would cry out" (Luke 19:40). I like to think Jesus was right. I like to think that the cross on the wall of this room where we memorialize Susan Angell, that the marks on her gravestone, that even the shrubs and trees and rocks where we will leave her, all in unison declare, "God loves her. Christ died for her. She is in God's hands."

Paul says, "At present we only see the baffling reflections in a mirror, but then it will be face to face" (1 Corinthians 13:12). To be face to face with God is to be face to face with what Dante in the last canto of the *Paradise* calls "the love that turns the sun and all the stars."

When the Waters Are Deep

J. HOWARD EDINGTON

Howard Edington's son John David accidentally drove his car into a tree in a rainstorm four days before Christmas, when he was twenty-two years old. The sermon itself tells the story, but focuses on the apostle Paul's assertion that faith, hope, and love endure when everything else in life is fragile and uncertain.

Howard Edington was for many years pastor of the First Presbyterian Church of Orlando, Florida, where he preached this sermon soon after John David's death. Today he is pastor of Providence Presbyterian Church in Hilton Head, South Carolina.

When the Waters Are Deep

1 CORINTHIANS 13:13

So faith, hope, love abide, these three; but the greatest of these is love.

1 CORINTHIANS 13:13

King David once said, "There is but one step between me and death."

Just one step. Tell me about it. On a stormy night, in the first hours of December 21, my son, my only son, John David, took that one step. On streets made slick by driving rain, he lost control of his car and crashed into a tree. In an instant, the candle of a life that had burned for twenty-two years was snuffed out. "There is but one step between me and death," King David said. Just one step.

The telephone ringing jolted us out of a deep sleep. The voice on the other end said, "There are Orlando policemen at your door, please let them in." Foreboding began to rise like floodwaters about us. Out of the rain and into our kitchen stepped a police officer and the police chaplain. The chaplain's name is Barry Henson. He also serves as a pastor at the Life Center Church in Eatonville. He is a man I had known and respected in recent years, but that night I came to love him. He came delivering the worst news any parent could ever hear, and yet he did it with such care and sensitivity. I shall never forget what he said and what he did. Very gently, he said, "There has been a terrible automobile accident, and your son did not survive." He then told us what they knew of the circumstances. Then he embraced us in his great, strong, loving arms and prayed a deeply moving prayer. With his message, our hearts were shattered, but with his prayer, our broken hearts began the long, slow, still-continuing process of mending.

I would like to share with you some things I've learned all over again through the death of my son. Yes, I've learned all over again that life is uncertain, that we are just one step away from death. But I've also learned all over again that in the midst of life's uncertainty there are some things that last: faith, hope, and love.

I've learned all over again that, while life is uncertain, faith lasts.

It was the toughest thing I have ever had to do. I had to go down to the medical examiner's office to provide positive identification of my son. Thankfully, my friends, Dr. John Tolson and Dr. Buck Brown, went with me. As I looked at the lifeless face of my son, his eyelids now closed in death, I said, "It's over, but it's not over." Yes, his life on this earth was over. There was no denying that, and there was no denying the pain of that.

Upon seeing her brother, his life now over, our daughter Meg Edington Sefton's love for her brother and love for language coalesced into some lines that poured out of her heart and rubbed up against my own feelings. She wrote,

No life. I can't believe it. No blood pumping through all those tiny veins of your hand. I am in shock. No life. How can that be? When I looked at you there, it was as if all time had stopped, all time had come to a halt. All those molecules, all those atoms, all those neutrons and electrons and protons that are supposedly in constant motion, were not moving, for there was literally no minute, no second, no split second, no nanosecond. You did not breathe. You did not sit up. You did not open your eyes. I expected you to sit up. I expected you to look at us with your blue eyes and sly smile and shyly say something cute, or softly ask us, "What's wrong?" or flippantly say, "I don't know what the big deal is; I'm just up here with God." But there you lay, in the fine mahogany box. You're wearing a powder blue necktie and a plaid jacket. Your hair is parted over too far and swept to the side just a bit too neatly. Your face is waxy and your long, fine nose seems more prominent than usual. Your hands are crossed just a bit too politely over your waist. I realize that the only time I would have seen you like this would have been in slumber. I realize that the only time I have seen you asleep was when you were a baby. It is only in dreams and in memories that I meet you now. I cry, but there is only the sound of my own echo.

I read your poetry and remember how I knew you. The thought that crossed my mind when I first found out was that I would never speak with you again. I thought of this, and the breath was taken out of me. I could not find the breath, and the silence crackled cold and hard, a sheet of ice across what is now an ocean of space. My mouth stands open, gaping, speechless, a silent red gash.

Meg's words capture the terrible pain all of us felt. John David's life was over. But my faith would not leave it there. My faith added the phrase, "but it's not over." And there is no denying that, either. I shall see my son again.

It's over, but it's not over. I reflected on what I would have done in that circumstance if I had no faith. If all I had been able to say was, "It's over," then I think I might have gone mad or tried to take my own life. And I wondered how anyone could ever face that kind of tragedy without faith. Being able to say, "It's over, but it's not over" turned unbearable grief into bearable sorrow.

Some years ago, the great Scottish preacher Arthur John Gossip lost his wife to tragic and untimely death. When he returned to his pulpit, he preached an incredibly powerful sermon that ended with these words:

I don't think we need to be afraid of life. Our hearts are very frail, and there are places where the road is very steep and very lonely. But we have a wonderful God. And as Paul puts it, what can separate us from his love? Not death, he says immediately, pushing that aside at once as the most obvious of all impossibilities. No, not death. For I, standing here in the roaring of the Jordan, cold to the heart with its dreadful chill and very conscious of the terror of its rushing, I can call back to you who, one day in your time, will have to cross it: Be of good cheer, my friend, for I feel the bottom and it is sound.

That's the way I feel now. I don't preach from this pulpit a rose-colored glasses, health-and-wealth, pie-in-the-sky kind of faith. What I do here on Sunday morning is not some well-rehearsed, carefully scripted performance akin to the theatrical stage. I'm not up here to pander to my ego or to play word games with you. And don't dare try to tell me that I don't know what life in the real world is all about. Don't dare suggest that because I am a preacher I am somehow insulated and isolated from the real workings of our world. Dear friends, I have been to the bottom! I have been to where few of you ever have been or ever will be. I have been to where life hurts the most and cuts the deepest and hits the hardest. Therefore, listen to me when I tell you that faith in Jesus Christ is not some sideline pursuit, some pleasant diversion, some enjoyable hobby in your life. It's not something you give yourself to when it's convenient or when it helps you along your career track or when you want to appear respectable. It's not just a part of your life. You've got to see it as the center of your life, the foundation of your whole existence. Nothing else in your life really matters, nothing else in your life will last. When the police chaplain says, "Your son did not survive," I can tell you that you find out right then that the only thing you have left is faith. But because of my faith, I can say to you, "I feel the bottom, and it is sound." Faith lasts.

And I've learned all over again that
while life is uncertain, hope lasts.

William Sloane Coffin was, for a number of years, the minister of the Riverside Church in New York City. He and I come at the Christian faith from radically different theological perspectives, but we now share a common bond. In January of 1983, William Sloane Coffin's twenty-four-year-old son, Alex, lost control of his car on a rainy night in Boston and plunged into the Boston Harbor. Alex died in the accident. Dr. Coffin said of Alex that his son beat him at every game, and now had beaten him to the grave. What he then said made me realize that not only do we have a common bond, but we also have a common hope. He said, "I know that when Alex beat me to the grave, the finish line was not Boston Harbor in the middle of the night. If . . . a lamp went out, it was because, for him at least, the Dawn had come."[1]

I think I would have said it differently. My son didn't beat me to the grave; he beat me to heaven! But while William Sloane Coffin and I may look at the faith from different perspectives, we do share the same hope. For my son, too, the dawn has come.

It was John Calvin, our Presbyterian ancestor, who said, "What would become of us if we did not take our stand upon hope, if we did not move through the darkness of this world on the path which is illumined by the word and the spirit of our God?"

That's the hope on which I stand. And that hope was confirmed for me in a call I received from a young man named Robert Midden. I did not know him, but he called to

1. See p. 60 above.

let me know that he was following John David that night when the accident occurred. He told me that he immediately rushed over to the car, checked for a pulse, and found none. He said, "Your son died instantly." He then went on to say something that has simply confirmed the hope I hold so dear. He said, "I called the police, and then I waited until they arrived." He paused for a moment and then he spoke once more: "Dr. Edington, I am a Christian. I want you to know that I held your son and surrounded him with prayer until the police came." Do you have any idea what it means to me to know that when the dawn came for my son, there was a disciple of Jesus Christ there to pray him home?

Yes, what would become of us if we did not take our stand upon hope? What would become of us indeed? Hope lasts.

**And I've learned all over again that
while life is uncertain, love lasts.**

I've known all along that life is serious and we dare not treat it lightly. I've known all along that we dare not put off until tomorrow what should be done today because tomorrow may never come. More times than I want to remember, I've stood at the graveside to bury the very young. I remember the time when the cemetery echoed with the sound of a twenty-one-gun salute and with heels clicking to attention as young soldiers handed the flag to a mother, who just days before heard a representative from the Department of the Army say, "We regret to inform you that your son was killed in action near Khe Sanh." I remember the day when we carried out to the cemetery the body of a ten-year-old boy who had been struck by lightning in a terrible storm, and I don't know that I was ever able to answer his parents' question,

Why? I remember the time when I buried one of my best friends and his fourteen-year-old son. They were killed by a drunken driver, and I tried to preach and to pray as we placed them side by side in the cemetery, and I now know that I left a piece of my heart in that place. I remember just a few months ago Trisha and I flew to Texas to wrap our arms and hearts around a couple with whom we have shared life for twenty years, and I buried their son whose life had ended tragically after just twenty-four years. And, of course, I look back across my dozen years with you, remembering the young people in this congregation so bright and attractive and full of life, who have been cut down long before their time, and I've struggled for all I'm worth to try to help their families find a way to live on.

Now, I, too, have lost a son. That's why I go on to remember that God, our Father, had a son, and in great love, God gave that son to die for us. And God then sat by the grave of his only son and mourned awhile, until, on Easter, he gave to his son and to my son, and to all of us, life eternal. His love lasts.

Therefore, my friends, the great tragedy in life is not to die, not even to die young. The great tragedy is to die without having lived. And the ultimate tragedy is to die without having lived with Christ and for Christ.

Back when the five of us in the Edington family were in the Holy Land, one of the things that we did was to drive to the top of Mount Tabor, known as the Mount of Transfiguration, not far from Nazareth. The road to the top was terribly narrow and filled with treacherous curves. Our driver seemed determined for some reason, known only to him, to get us to the top in record time, and as a result, we went careening along this treacherous road, flirting with disaster the whole way. I was in the front seat, Trisha and the kids were in the back. Suddenly in the midst of this wild ride, John David leaned up and said, "Dad, let me have that little Bible you always carry in your pocket." I said, "Why?" He replied, "Because I think we're going to die on this mountain, and when I die I want to be reading the Bible so that God will know I belong to him." Needless to say, I handed him my Bible! We've always loved telling that story in our family. But, of course, God already knew that John David was his. You see, God so loved John David that he gave his only begotten son. The death of my son hurts. The wound is deep, but the wound is clean. For I know how I loved him, and how he loved me, and how God loves the both of us.

If you don't hear anything else in this sermon, please hear this; if you don't remember anything else from this worship service, please remember this; if you don't do anything else in response to this experience, please do this: love while you still can love. Make the most of any moments that are yours, because too soon they may be gone. Then you will be left with nothing but your memories. So build good memories in your life. I plead with you today, in the name of Jesus Christ, love: Love those whom God has given you to love and love them while you still can. I did that. And now I am so glad. Love lasts.

I have been helped in recent days by recalling that in the year 1873, H. G. Spafford, a Christian lawyer from Chicago, placed his wife and four children on the ocean liner *Ville du Havre*, sailing from New York to France. Spafford expected to join them three weeks later, after finishing up some business at home. The trip started beautifully, but on the evening of November 21, 1873, as the *Ville du Havre* plowed through the waters of the Atlantic, the ship was suddenly struck by another vessel, the *Lochearn*. Thirty minutes later, the *Ville du Havre* sank, with the loss of nearly all on board. Mrs. Spafford was rescued by the sailors of the *Lochearn*, but the four children were gone. Mrs. Spafford then wired a message to her husband. It read, "Saved alone." That night Spafford walked the floors of his rooms in anguish, but also in prayer. Toward morning, he told a friend named Major Whittle, "I'm glad to be able to trust my Lord when it costs me something." Several weeks later, Spafford sailed from New York to join his grieving wife on the other side of the Atlantic. As his ship crossed the precise spot in the ocean where the *Ville du Havre* had gone down, carrying his children to their death, he sat down and wrote a hymn. The words he wrote were eventually set to Philip Bliss's tune, named for the ship on which Spafford's children died, *Ville du Havre*. The words he wrote have strengthened many a soul, and now they are strengthening mine.

> When peace, like a river, attendeth my way,
> When sorrows like sea billows roll;
> Whatever my lot,
> Thou hast taught me to say,
> It is well, it is well with my soul.

Dear friends, it is costing me dearly to say this to you, but when the waters are deep in your life, when sorrows like sea billows roll, you can say, and know it will be true: In Christ, it is well, it is well with my soul. Amen.

True Saints,
When Absent from the Body,
Are Present with the Lord

....

JONATHAN EDWARDS

Those who care about the legacy of Jonathan Edwards might well wish that his reputation as a preacher were established on the foundation of this sermon rather than on the less typical "Sinners in the Hands of an Angry God." Edwards was able to preach hellfire with a cool head, and believed it was rational to do so, in light of what he believed about hell. His approach, however, was more typically to try to move the affections of his hearers with a sense of the beauty of spiritual realities.

David Brainerd died of tuberculosis in the Edwards home in Northampton, Massachusetts, on October 9, 1747, and was buried in the Edwards family plot. In life Brainerd was an undistinguished student, and death ended his pastoral and missionary work almost before it had begun. In editing and publishing Brainerd's diary, however, Edwards constructed a riveting, literary Brainerd who had immense influence on American evangelical self-understanding.[1]

---

1. See Norman Pettit, "Editor's Introduction," in *Works of Jonathan Edwards,* vol. 7: *The Life of David Brainerd* (New Haven: Yale University Press, 1985), pp. 1-85.

Two weeks after Brainerd's funeral, Edwards had the vastly more difficult responsibility of preaching a funeral sermon for one of his own daughters. Jerusha Edwards had nursed David Brainerd through his illness, and when she died two weeks after he did, she was buried beside him. Edwards's funeral sermon for Jerusha is forthcoming in the Yale edition of Edwards's works.

This new abridgement of the sermon for David Brainerd's funeral presented here was prepared by Kenneth P. Minkema, director of the Works of Jonathan Edwards project at Yale University.

True Saints,
When Absent from the Body,
Are Present with the Lord

2 CORINTHIANS 5:8

We are confident, I say, and willing rather to be absent from the body, and to be present with the Lord.

2 CORINTHIANS 5:8

The Apostle in this place is giving a reason why he went on with so much boldness and immovable steadfastness, through such labors, sufferings, and dangers of his life, in the service of his Lord, for which his enemies, the false teachers among the Corinthians, sometimes reproached him as being beside himself, and driven on by a kind of madness. — In the latter part of the preceding chapter, the Apostle informs the Christian Corinthians that the reason why he did thus was that he firmly believed the promises that Christ had made to his faithful servants of a glorious future eternal reward, and knew that these present afflictions were light, and but for a moment, in comparison of that far more exceeding and eternal weight of glory. The same discourse is continued in this chapter, wherein the

81

Apostle further insists on the reason he had given of his constancy in suffering, and exposing himself to death in the work of the ministry, even the more happy state he expected after death. And this is the subject of the text, wherein may be observed:

1. The great future privilege, which the Apostle hoped for: that of being present with Christ. The words in the original properly signify dwelling with Christ, as in the same country or city, or making a home with Christ.

2. When the Apostle looked for this privilege, viz., when he should be absent from the body. Not to wait for it till the resurrection, when soul and body should be united again. He signifies the same thing in his epistle to the Philippians, chapter 1:22, 23: "But if I live in the flesh, this is the fruit of my labor. Yet what I shall choose, I wot not. For I am in a strait between two; having a desire to depart, and to be with Christ."

3. The value the Apostle set on this privilege. It was such that for the sake of it, he chose to be absent from the body. He was willing rather, or (as the word properly signifies) it were more pleasing to him, to part with the present life, and all its enjoyments, for the sake of being possessed of this great benefit.

4. The present benefit, which the Apostle had, by his faith and hope of this future privilege, viz., that hence he received courage, assurance, and constancy of mind: agreeable to the proper import of the word that is rendered, "we are confident." The Apostle is now giving a reason of that fortitude and immovable stability of mind with which he went through those extreme labors, hardships, and dangers, which he mentions in this discourse. So that in the

midst of all he did not faint, was not discouraged, but had constant light, and inward support, strength, and comfort in the midst of all: agreeable to the sixteenth verse of the foregoing chapter [2 Corinthians 4], "For which cause, we faint not; but though our outward man perish, yet the inward man is renewed day by day." And the same is expressed more particularly in the eighth, ninth, and tenth verses of that chapter, "We are troubled on every side, yet not distressed; we are perplexed, but not in despair; persecuted, but not forsaken; cast down, but not destroyed; always bearing about in the body, the dying of the Lord Jesus, that the life also of Jesus might be made manifest in our mortal flesh." And in the next chapter [chapter 6], verses 4-10: "In all things approving ourselves as the ministers of God, in much patience, in afflictions, in necessities, in distresses, in stripes, in imprisonments, in tumults, in labors, in watchings, in fastings, by pureness; by knowledge, by long-suffering, by kindness, by the Holy Ghost, by love unfeigned, by the word of truth, by the power of God, by the armor of righteousness on the right hand and on the left, by honor and dishonor, by evil report and good report: as deceivers, and yet true; as unknown, and yet well known; as dying, and behold, we live; as chastened, and not killed; as sorrowful, yet always rejoicing; as poor, yet making many rich; as having nothing, and yet possessing all things."

Among the many useful observations there might be raised from the text, I shall at this time only insist on that which lies most plainly before us in the words, viz., *The souls of true saints, when they leave their bodies at death, go to be with Christ.*

The souls of true saints go to be with Christ, in the following respects:

1. They go to dwell in the same blessed abode with the glorified human nature of Christ:

The human nature of Christ is yet in being. He still continues, and will continue to all eternity, to be both God and man. His whole human nature remains: not only his human soul, but also his human body. His dead body rose from the dead, and the same that was raised from the dead, is exalted and glorified at God's right hand; that which was dead is now alive and lives for evermore.

And therefore there is a certain place, a particular part of the external creation, to which Christ is gone, and where he remains. And this place is that which we call the highest heaven, or the heaven of heavens, a place beyond all the visible heavens, Ephesians 4:9, 10. . . . And they are elsewhere often represented as before the throne of God, or surrounding his throne in heaven, and sent from thence, and descending from thence on messages to this world. And thither it is that the souls of departed saints are conducted when they die. They are not reserved in some abode distinct from the highest heaven: a place of rest, which they are kept in till the day of judgment, such as some imagine, which they call the *hades* of the happy. But they go directly to heaven itself. This is the saints' home, being their Father's house: they are pilgrims and strangers on the earth, and this is the other and better country to which they are traveling, Hebrews 11:13-26. This is the city they belong to; Philippians 3:20, "Our conversation (or as the word properly signifies, citizenship) is in heaven." Therefore this undoubtedly is the place the Apostle has respect to in my text, when he says, "We are willing to forsake our former house, the body, and to dwell in the same house, city, or country, wherein Christ dwells"; which is the proper import of the original. What can this house, or city, or country be, but that house, which is elsewhere spoken of as their proper home, and their Father's house, and the city and country to which they properly belong, and whither they are traveling all the while they continue in this world, and the house, city, and country where we know the human nature of Christ is? This is the saints' rest: here their hearts are while they live, and here their treasure is. . . .

2. The souls of true saints, when they leave their bodies at death, go to be with Christ, as they go to dwell in the immediate, full, and constant sight or view of him.

When we are absent from our dear friends, they are out of sight, but when we are with them, we have the opportunity and satisfaction of seeing them. So while the saints are in the body, and are absent from the Lord, he is in several respects out of sight, 1 Peter 1:8, "Whom having not seen, ye love: in whom, though now ye see him not, yet believing," etc. They have indeed, in this world, a spiritual sight of Christ, but they see through a glass darkly, and with great interruption, but in heaven they see him face to face, 1 Corinthians 13:12. "The pure in heart are blessed; for they shall see God," Matthew 5:8. Their beatific vision of God is in Christ, who is that brightness or effulgence of God's glory, by which his glory shines forth in heaven, to the view of saints and angels there, as well as here on earth. This is the Sun of righteousness that is not only the light of this world, but is also the sun that enlightens the heavenly Jerusalem, by whose bright beams it is that the glory of God shines forth there, to the enlightening and making happy all the glorious inhabitants. . . . They have a most clear view of the unfathomable depths of the manifold wisdom and knowledge of God, and the most bright displays of the infinite purity and holiness of God which appear in that way and work, and see in another manner than the saints do here, what is the breadth and length, and depth and height, of the grace and love of Christ, appearing in his redemption. And as they see the unspeakable riches and glory of the attribute of God's grace, so they most clearly behold and understand Christ's eternal and unmeasurable dying love to them in particular. And in short, they see everything in Christ that tends to kindle, enflame, and gratify love, and everything that tends to satisfy them, and that in the most clear and glorious manner, without any darkness or delusion, without any impediment or interruption. Now the saints, while in the body, see something of Christ's glory and love, as in the dawning of the morning, we see something of the reflected light of the sun mingled with darkness. But when separated from the body, they see their glorious and loving Redeemer, as we see the sun when risen, and showing his whole disk above the horizon, by his direct beams, in a clear hemisphere, and with perfect day.

3. The souls of true saints, when absent from the body, go to be with Jesus Christ, as they are brought into a most perfect conformity to and union with him.

Their spiritual conformity is begun while they are in the body. Here beholding as in a glass the glory of the Lord, they are changed into the same image. But when they come to see him as he is, in heaven, then they become like him in another manner. That perfect sight will abolish all remains of deformity, disagreement, and sinful unlikeness, as all darkness is abolished before the full blaze of the sun's meridian light. As it is impossible that the least degree of obscurity should remain before such light, so it is impossible the least degree of sin and spiritual deformity should remain with such a view of the spiritual beauty and glory of Christ, as the saints enjoy in heaven, when they see that Sun of righteousness without a cloud. They themselves shall not only shine forth as the sun, but shall be as little suns, without a spot. For then is come the time when Christ presents his saints to himself, in glorious beauty; "not having spot, or wrinkle, or any such thing"; and having holiness without a blemish. . . .

4. Departed souls of saints are with Christ, as they enjoy a glorious and immediate intercourse and converse with him.

While we are present with our friends, we have opportunity for that free and immediate conversation with them, which we cannot have in absence from them. And therefore, by reason of the vastly more free, perfect, and immediate intercourse with Christ, which the saints enjoy when absent from the body, they are fitly represented as present with him.

The most intimate intercourse becomes that relation which the saints stand in to Jesus Christ; and especially becomes that most perfect and glorious union they shall be brought into with him in heaven. . . . When they go to heaven where he is, they are exalted and glorified with him, and shall not be kept at a more awful distance from Christ, but shall be admitted nearer, and to a greater intimacy. For they shall be unspeakably more fit for it, and Christ in more fit circumstances to bestow on them this blessedness. Their seeing the great glory of their friend and Redeemer, will not awe them to a distance, and make them afraid of a near approach, but on the contrary, will most powerfully draw them near, and encourage and engage them to holy freedom. For they will know that it is he that is their own Redeemer, and beloved friend and bridegroom: the very same that loved them with a dying love, and redeemed them to God by his blood. . . . And accordingly the souls of departed saints with Christ in heaven, shall have Christ as it were unbosomed unto them, manifesting those infinite riches of love toward them, that have been there from eternity. They shall be enabled to express their love to him, in an incomparably better manner than ever they could while in the body. Thus they shall eat and drink abundantly, and swim in the ocean of love, and be eternally swallowed up in the infinitely bright, and infinitely mild and sweet beams of divine love: eternally receiving that light, eternally full of it, and eternally compassed round with it, and everlastingly reflecting it back again to the fountain of it.

5. The souls of the saints, when they leave their bodies at death, go to be with Christ, as they are received to a glorious fellowship with Christ in his blessedness.

As the wife is received to a joint possession of her husband's estate, and as the wife of a prince partakes with him in his princely possessions and honors, so the church, the spouse of Christ, when the marriage comes, and she is received to dwell with him in heaven, shall partake with him in his glory. When Christ rose from the dead, and took possession of eternal life, this was not as a private person, but as the public head of all his redeemed people. He took possession of it for them, as well as for himself, and they are "quickened together with him, and raised up together." — And so when he ascended into heaven, and was exalted to great glory there, this also was as a public person. He took possession of heaven, not only for himself, but his people, as their forerunner and head, that they might ascend also, "and sit together in heavenly places with him," Ephesians 2:5, 6, "Christ writes upon them his new name," Revelation 3:12; i.e., he makes them partakers of his own glory and exaltation in heaven. His new name is that new honor and glory that the Father invested him with, when he set him on his own right hand, as a prince, when he advances anyone to new dignity in his kingdom, gives him a new title. Christ and his saints shall be glorified together, Romans 8:17.

The saints in heaven have communion, or a joint participation with Christ in his glory and blessedness in heaven, in the following respects more especially.

First, they partake with him in the ineffable delights he has in heaven, in the enjoyment of his Father.

When Christ ascended into heaven, he was received to a glorious and peculiar joy and blessedness in the enjoyment of his Father, who in his passion hid his face from him — such an enjoyment as became the relation he stood in to the Father, and such as was a meet reward for the great and hard service he had performed on earth. Then "God showed him the path of life, and brought him into his presence, where is fullness of joy, and to sit on his right hand, where there are pleasures for evermore," as Psalm 16:11. . . . The saints shall have pleasure in partaking with Christ in his pleasure, and shall see light in his light. They shall partake with Christ of the same river of pleasure, shall drink of the same water of life, and of the same new wine in the Father's kingdom, Matthew 26:29. That new wine is especially that joy and happiness that Christ and his true disciples shall partake of together in glory, which is the purchase of Christ's blood, or the reward of his obedience unto death. Christ, at his ascension into heaven, received everlasting pleasures at his Father's right hand, and in the enjoyment of his love, as the reward of his own death, or obedience unto death. But the same righteousness is reckoned to both head and members. Both shall have fellowship in the same reward, each according to their distinct capacity.

That the saints in heaven have such a communion with Christ in his joy, and do so partake with him in his own enjoyment of the Father, greatly manifests the transcendent excellency of their happiness, and their being admitted to a vastly higher privilege in glory than the angels.

Second, the saints in heaven are received to a fellowship or participation with Christ in the glory of that dominion to which the Father has exalted him.

The saints, when they ascend to heaven as Christ ascended, and are made to sit together with Christ in heavenly places, and are partakers of the glory of his exaltation, are exalted to reign with him. They are through him made kings and priests, and reign with him, and in him, over the same kingdom. As the Father has appointed unto him a kingdom, so he has appointed to them. The Father has appointed the Son to reign over his own kingdom, and the Son appoints his saints to reign in his. . . . Such is the saints' union with Christ, and their interest in him, that what he possesses they possess, in a much more perfect and blessed manner than if all things were given to them separately, and by themselves, to be disposed of according to their discretion. They are now disposed of so as, in every respect, to be most for their blessedness, by an infinitely better discretion than their own, and in being disposed of by their head and husband, between whom and them there is the most perfect union of hearts, and the most perfect union of wills. . . .

Third, the departed souls of saints have fellowship with Christ, in his blessed and eternal employment of glorifying the Father.

The happiness of heaven consists not only in contemplation, and a mere passive enjoyment, but consists very much in action. And particularly in actively serving and glorifying God. This is expressly mentioned as a great part of the blessedness of the saints in their most perfect state, Revelation 22:3, "And there shall be no more curse; but the throne of God and of the Lamb shall be in it; and his servants shall serve him." The angels are as a flame of fire in their ardor and activity in God's service. The four animals, Revelation 4 (which are generally supposed to signify the angels), are represented as continually giving praise and glory to God, and are said not to rest day nor night, verse 8. The souls of departed saints are, doubtless, become as the angels of God in heaven in this respect. And Jesus Christ is the head of the whole glorious assembly, as in other things appertaining to their blessed state, so in this of their praising and glorifying the Father. When Christ, the night before he was crucified, prayed for his exaltation to glory, it was that he might glorify the Father, John 17:1, "These words spake Jesus, and lift up his eyes to heaven, and said, Father, the hour is come, glorify thy Son, that thy Son also may glorify thee." And this he doubtless does, now [that] he is in heaven, not only in fulfilling the Father's will, in what he does as Head of the church and Ruler of the universe, but also in leading the heavenly assembly in their praises. When Christ instituted the Lord's Supper, and ate and drank with his disciples at his table (giving them therein a representation and pledge of their future feasting with him, and drinking new wine in his heavenly Father's kingdom), he at that time led them in their praises to God, in a hymn they sang. And so doubtless he leads his glorified disciples in heaven. David was the sweet psalmist of Israel, and he led the great congregation of God's people in their songs of praise. Herein, as well as in innumerable other things, he was a type of Christ, who is often spoken of in Scripture by the name of David. And many of the psalms that David penned, were songs of praise that he, by the spirit of prophecy, uttered in the name of Christ, as head of the church, and leading the saints in their praises. Christ in heaven leads the glorious assembly in their praises to God, as Moses did the congregation of Israel at the Red Sea, which is implied in its being said that "they sing the song of Moses and the Lamb," Revelation 15:2, 3. In Revelation 19:5, John tells us that "he heard a voice come out of the throne, saying, Praise our God, all ye his servants, and ye that fear him, both small and great." Who can it be that utters this voice out of the throne, but the Lamb that is in the midst of the throne, calling on the glorious assembly of saints to praise his Father and their Father, his God and their God? And what the consequence of this voice is, we have an account in the next words: "And I heard as it were the voice of a great multitude, and as the voice of many waters, and as the voice of mighty thunderings, saying Alleluia; for the Lord God omnipotent reigneth."

The use that I would make of what has been said on this subject is of *exhortation*. Let us all be exhorted hence earnestly to seek after that great privilege, that when "we are absent from the body, we may be present with the Lord." We cannot continue always in these earthly tabernacles; — they are very frail, and will soon decay and fall, and are continually liable to be overthrown by innumerable means. Our souls must soon leave them, and go into the eternal world. — O, how infinitely great will the privilege and happiness of such be, who at that time shall go to be with Christ in his glory, in the manner that has been represented! The privilege of the twelve disciples was great, in being so constantly with Christ as his family, in his state of humiliation. The privilege of those three disciples was great, who were with him in the mount of his transfiguration, where was exhibited to them some little semblance of his future glory in heaven, such as they might behold in the present frail, feeble, and sinful state. They were greatly entertained and delighted with what they saw, and were for making tabernacles to dwell there, and return no more down the mount. And great was the privilege of Moses when he was with Christ in mount Sinai, and besought him to show him his glory, and he saw his back parts as he passed by, and proclaimed his name. — But how infinitely greater the privilege of being with Christ in heaven, where he sits on the right hand of God, as the glory of the King and God of angels, and of the whole universe, shining forth as the great light, the bright sun of that world of glory; there to dwell in the full, constant, and everlasting view of his beauty and brightness; there most freely and intimately to converse with him, and fully to enjoy his love, as his friends and spouse; there to have fellowship with him in the infinite pleasure and joy he has in the enjoyment of his Father! How transcendent the privilege, there to sit with him on his throne, to reign with him in the possession of all things, and partake with him in the joy and glory of his victory over his enemies, and the advancement of his kingdom in the world, and to join with him in joyful songs of praise to his Father and their Father, to his God and their God, forever and ever! Is not such a privilege worth seeking after?

But here, as a special enforcement of this exhortation, I would improve that dispensation of God's holy providence, which is the sorrowful occasion of our coming together at this time, viz., the death of that eminent servant of Jesus Christ, in the work of the gospel-ministry, whose funeral is this day to be attended; together with what was observable in him, living and dying.

In this dispensation of Providence, God puts us in mind of our mortality, and forewarns us that the time is approaching when we must be absent from the body, and "must all appear (as the Apostle observes in the context) before the judgment seat of Christ, that every one of us may receive the things done in the body, according to what we have done, whether it be good or bad."

And in him, whose death we are now called to consider and improve, we have not only an instance of mortality, but an instance of one that, being absent from the body, is present with the Lord, as we have all imaginable reason to conclude. And that whether we consider the nature of the operations he was under, about the time whence he dates his conversion, or the nature and course of his inward exercises from that time forward, or his outward conversation and practices in life, or his frame and behavior during the whole of that long season wherein he looked death in the face.

His convictions of sin, preceding his first consolations in Christ (as appears by a written account he has left of his inward exercises and experiences), were exceeding deep and thorough. His trouble and exercise of mind, through a sense of guilt and misery, very great and long-continued, but yet sound and solid, consist[ed] in no unsteady, violent, and unaccountable hurries and frights, and strange perturbations of mind, but [arose] from the most serious consideration, and proper illumination of the conscience to discern and consider the true state of things. And the light let into his mind at conversion, and the influences and exercises that his mind was subject to at that time, appear very agreeable to reason and the gospel of Jesus Christ. The change [was] very great and remarkable, without any appearance of strong impressions on the imagination, sudden flights and pangs of the affections, and vehement emotions in animal nature, but attended with proper intellectual views of the supreme glory of the Divine Being, consisting in the infinite dignity and beauty of the perfections of his nature, and of the transcendent excellency of the way of salvation by Christ. — This was about eight years ago, when he was about twenty-one years of age.

Thus God sanctified and made meet for his use, that vessel which he intended to make of eminent honor in his house, and which he had made of large capacity, having endowed him with very uncommon abilities and gifts of nature. He was a singular instance of a ready invention, natural eloquence, easy flowing expression, sprightly apprehension, quick discerning, and a very strong memory, and yet of a very penetrating genius, close and clear thought, and piercing judgment. He had an exact taste. His understanding was quick, strong, and distinguishing.

His learning was very considerable, for which he had a great taste, and applied himself to his studies in so close a manner when he was at college, that he much injured his health, and was obliged on that account for a while to leave his studies and return home. He was esteemed one that excelled in learning in that society.

He had an extraordinary knowledge of men, as well as things, had a great insight into human nature, and excelled most that ever I knew in a communicative faculty. He had a peculiar talent at accommodating himself to the capacities, tempers, and circumstances of those whom he would instruct or counsel.

He had extraordinary gifts for the pulpit. I never had opportunity to hear him preach, but have often heard him pray. I think his manner of addressing himself to God, and expressing himself before him, in that duty, almost inimitable, such (so far as I may judge) as I have very rarely known equaled. He expressed himself with that exact propriety and pertinency, in such significant, weighty, pungent expressions, with that decent appearance of sincerity, reverence, and solemnity, and great distance from all affectation, as forgetting the presence of men, and as being in the immediate presence of a great and holy God, that I have scarcely ever known paralleled. And his manner of preaching, by what I have often heard of it from good judges, was no less excellent: being clear and instructive, natural, nervous, forcible, and moving, and very searching and convincing. — He rejected with disgust an affected noisiness, and violent boisterousness in the pulpit, and yet much disrelished a flat, cold delivery, when the subject of discourse, and matter delivered, required affection and earnestness.

Not only had he excellent talents for the study and the pulpit, but also for conversation. He was of a sociable disposition and was remarkably free, entertaining, and profitable in ordinary discourse, and had much of a faculty of disputing, defending truth and confuting error.

As he excelled in his judgment and knowledge of things in general, so especially in divinity. He was truly, for one of his standing, an extraordinary divine. But above all, in matters relating to experimental religion. In this, I know I have the concurring opinion of some who have had a name for persons of the best judgment. And according to what ability I have to judge things of this nature, and according to my opportunities, which of late have been very great, I never knew his equal, of his age and standing, for clear, accurate notions of the nature and essence of true religion, and its distinctions from its various false appearances, which I suppose to be owing to these three things meeting together in him: the strength of his natural genius, the great opportunities he had of observing others, in various parts, both white people and Indians, and his own great experience.

His experiences of the holy influences of God's Spirit were not only great at his first conversion, but they were so in a continued course, from that time forward, as appears by a private journal which he kept of his daily inward exercises from the time of his conversion until he was disabled by the failing of his strength, a few days before his death. The change which he looked upon as his conversion, was not merely a great change of the *present* views, affections, and frame of his mind, but also the beginning of that work of God on his heart, which God *carried on* from that time to his dying day. He greatly abhorred the way of such as live on their first work, as though they had now got through their work, and are thenceforward, by degrees, settled in a cold, lifeless, negligent, worldly frame. He had an ill opinion of such persons' religion.

His experiences were very diverse from many things that have lately obtained the reputation, with multitudes, of the very height of Christian experience. About the time that the false religion, which arises chiefly from impressions on the imagination, began first to make a very great appearance in the land, he was for a little while deceived with it, so as to think highly of it. And though he knew he never had such experiences as others told of, he thought it was because others' attainments were beyond his, and so coveted them and sought after them but could never obtain them. He told me that he never had what is called an impulse, or a strong impression of his imagination, in things of religion, in his life. But [he] owned that during the short time that he thought well of these things, he was tinged with that spirit of false zeal that is wont to attend them. But said that then he was not in his element, but as a fish out of water. And when, after a little while, he came clearly to see the vanity and perniciousness of such things[,] [i]t cost him abundance of sorrow and distress of mind, and to my knowledge he afterwards freely and openly confessed the errors in conduct that he had run into, and laid himself low before them whom he had offended. And since his conviction of his error in those respects, he has ever had a peculiar abhorrence of that kind of bitter zeal, and those delusive experiences that have been the principal source of it. He detested enthusiasm in all its forms and operations, and abhorred whatever in opinion or experience seemed to verge towards antinomianism, as the experiences of those whose first faith consists in believing that Christ died for them in particular, and their first love, in loving God, because they supposed they were the objects of his love. Their assurance of their good estate [was] from some immediate testimony or suggestion, either with or without texts of Scripture, that their sins are forgiven, that God loves them, etc., and the joys of such as rejoiced more in their own supposed distinction from others, in honor, and privileges, and high experiences, than in God's excellency and Christ's beauty: the spiritual pride of such laymen, [who] are for setting up themselves as public teachers, and cry down human learning, and a learned ministry. He greatly disliked a disposition in persons to much noise and show in religion, and affecting to be abundant in publishing and proclaiming their own experience. Though he did not condemn, but approved of Christians speaking of their experiences, on some occasions, and to some persons, with modesty, discretion, and reserve. He abominated the spirit and practice of the generality of the Separatists in this land. I heard him say, once and again, that he had been much with this kind of people, and was acquainted with many of them, in various parts, and that by this acquaintance, he knew that what was chiefly and most generally in repute amongst them, as the power of godliness, was entirely a different thing from that vital piety recommended in the Scripture, and had nothing in it of that nature. He never was more full in condemning these things than in his last illness, and after he ceased to have any expectation of life. [This was] particularly when he had the greatest and nearest views of approaching eternity, and several times, when he thought himself actually dying, and expected in a few minutes to be in the eternal world, as he himself told me.

As his inward experiences appear to have been of the right kind, and were very remarkable as to their degree, so was his outward behavior and practice agreeable. He in his whole course acted as one who had indeed sold all for Christ, and had entirely devoted himself to God, and made his glory his highest end, and was fully determined to spend his whole time and strength in his service. He was lively in religion, in the right way: lively, not only, nor chiefly, with his tongue, in professing and talking, but lively in the work and business of religion. He was not one of those who are for contriving ways to shun the cross, and get to heaven with ease and sloth, but was such an instance of one living a life of labor and self-denial, and spending his strength and substance in pursuing that great end, and the glory of his Redeemer, that perhaps is scarcely to be paralleled in this age in these parts of the world. Much of this may be perceived by anyone that reads his printed journal, but much more has been learned by long intimate acquaintance with him, and by looking into his diary since his death, which he purposely concealed in what he published.

And as his desires and labors for the advancement of Christ's kingdom were great, so was his success. God was pleased to make him the instrument of bringing to pass the most remarkable things among the poor savages — in enlightening, awakening, reforming, and changing their disposition and manners, and wonderfully transforming them — that perhaps can be produced in these latter ages of the world. An account of this has been given the public in his journals, drawn up by order of the Honorable Society in

Scotland, that employed him, which I would recommend to the perusal of all such as take pleasure in the wonderful works of God's grace, and would read that which will peculiarly tend both to entertain and profit a Christian mind.

No less extraordinary than the things already mentioned of him in life, was his constant calmness, peace, assurance, and joy in God, during the long time he looked death in the face, without the least hope of recovery: continuing without interruption to the last, while his distemper very sensibly preyed upon his vitals, from day to day, and oft brought him to that state in which he looked upon himself, and was thought by others, to be dying. The thoughts of approaching death never seemed in the least to damp, but rather to encourage him, and exhilarate his mind. And the nearer death approached, the more desirous he seemed to be of it. He said, not long before his death, that "the consideration of the day of death, and the day of judgment, had a long time been peculiarly sweet to him." And at another time, that "he could not but think of the meetness there was in throwing such a rotten carcass as his into the grave: it seemed to him to be the right way of disposing of it." He often used the epithet *glorious*, when speaking of the day of his death, calling it *that glorious day*. On a sabbath day morning, September 27, feeling an unusual appetite to food, and looking on it as a sign of approaching death, he said, "he should look on it as a favor, if this might be his dying day, and he longed for the time." He had before expressed himself desirous of seeing his brother again, whose return had been expected from the Jerseys, but then (speaking of him) he said, "I am willing to go, and never see him again: I care not what I part with, to be for ever with the Lord." Being asked, that morning, how he did? He answered, "I am almost in eternity: God knows, I long to be there. My work is done; I have done with all my friends; all the world is nothing to me." On the evening of the next day, when he thought himself dying, and was apprehended to be so by others, and he could utter himself only by broken whispers, he often repeated the word *Eternity*; and said, "I shall soon be with the holy angels. — He will come; he will not tarry." He told me one night, as he went to bed, that "he expected to die that night." And added, "I am not at all afraid, I am willing to go this night, if it be the will of God. Death is what I long for." He sometimes expressed himself as "nothing to do but to die: and being willing to go that minute, if it was the will of God." He sometimes used that expression, "O why is his chariot so long in coming."

He seemed to have remarkable exercises of resignation to the will of God. He once told me that "he had longed for the outpouring of the Holy Spirit of God, and the glorious times of the church, and hoped they were coming; and should have been willing to have lived to promote religion at that time, if that had been the will of God. But (says he) I am willing it should be as it is: I would not have the choice to make myself for ten thousand worlds."

He several times spoke of the different kinds of willingness to die, and spoke of it as an ignoble mean kind, to be willing, only to get rid of pain, or to go to heaven only to get honor and advancement there. His own longings for death seemed to be quite of a different kind, and for nobler ends. When he was first taken with something like a diarrhea, which is looked upon as one of the last and most fatal symptoms in a consumption, he said, "O now the glorious time is coming? I have longed to serve God perfectly; and God will gratify these desires." And at one time and another, in the latter part of his illness, he uttered these expressions. "My heaven is to please God, and glorify him, and give all to him, and to be wholly devoted to his glory. — That is the heaven I long for. That is my religion, and that is my happiness, and always was, ever since I supposed I had any true religion. All those that are of that religion, shall meet me in heaven. I do not go to heaven to be advanced, but to give honor to God. It is no matter where I shall be stationed in heaven, whether I have a high or low seat there, but to love, and please, and glorify God. If I had a thousand souls, if they were worth anything, I would give them all to God: but I have nothing to give, when all is done. It is impossible for any rational creature to be happy without acting all for God. God himself could not make me happy any other way. — I long to be in heaven, praising and glorifying God with the holy angels; all my desire is to glorify God. — My heart goes out to the burying place, it seems to me a desirable place: But O to glorify God! That is it! That is above all! — It is a great comfort to me to think that I have done a little for God in the world: It is but a very small matter; yet I have done a little; and I lament it, that I have not done more for him. — There is nothing in the world worth living for, but doing good, and finishing God's work, doing the work that Christ did. I see nothing else in the world that can yield any satisfaction, besides living to God, pleasing him, and doing his whole will. My greatest joy and comfort has been to do something for promoting the interest of religion, and the souls of particular persons."

After he came to be in so low a state, that he ceased to

have the least expectation of recovery, his mind was peculiarly carried forth with earnest concern for the prosperity of the church of God on earth, which seemed very manifestly to arise from a pure disinterested love to Christ, and desire of his glory. The prosperity of Zion was a theme he dwelt much upon, and of which he spoke much, and more and more, the nearer death approached. He told me when near his end, that "he never, in all his life, had his mind so led forth in desires and earnest prayers for the flourishing of Christ's kingdom on earth, as since he was brought so exceeding low at Boston." He seemed much to wonder that there appeared no more disposition in ministers and people to pray for the flourishing of religion through the world. And particularly, he several times expressed his wonder, that there appeared no more forwardness to comply with the proposal lately made from Scotland, for united extraordinary prayer among God's people, for the coming of Christ's kingdom, and sent it as his dying advice to his own congregation, that they should practice agreeably to that proposal.

A little before his death, he said to me, as I came into the room, "My thoughts have been employed on the old dear theme, the prosperity of God's church on earth. As I waked out of sleep (said he) I was led to cry for the pouring out of God's Spirit, and the advancement of Christ's kingdom, which the dear Redeemer did and suffered so much for: it is that especially makes me long for it." — But a few days before his death, he desired us to sing a psalm concerning the prosperity of Zion, which he signified his mind was engaged in above all things. At his desire we sang a part of the 102nd psalm. And when we had done, though he was then so low that he could scarcely speak, he so exerted himself, that he made a prayer, very audibly, wherein, besides praying for those present, and for his own congregation, he earnestly prayed for the reviving and flourishing of religion in the world. His own congregation especially lay much on his heart. He often spoke of them, and commonly when he did so, it was with extraordinary tenderness, so that his speech was interrupted and drowned with weeping.

Thus I have endeavored to represent something of the character and behavior of that excellent servant of Christ, whose funeral is now to be attended. Though I have done it very imperfectly; yet I have endeavored to do it faithfully, and as in the presence and fear of God, without flattery; which surely is to be abhorred in ministers of the gospel, when speaking as messengers of the Lord of Hosts. Such reason have we to be satisfied that the person spoken of, now he is absent from the body, is present with the Lord, and now wearing a crown of glory, of distinguished brightness.

And how much is there in the consideration of such an example, and so blessed an end, to excite us, who are yet alive, with the greatest diligence and earnestness, to improve the time of life, that we also may go to be with Christ, when we forsake the body! The time is coming, and will soon come, we know not how soon, when we must take leave of all things here below, to enter on a fixed unalterable state in the eternal world. O, how well is it worth the while to labor and suffer, and deny ourselves, to lay up in store a good foundation of support and supply, against that time! How much is such a peace as we have heard of, worth at such a time. And how dismal would it be, to be in such circumstances, under the outward distresses of a consuming, dissolving frame, and looking death in the face from day to day, with hearts uncleansed, and sin unpardoned, under a dreadful load of guilt and divine wrath, having much sorrow and wrath in our sickness, and nothing to comfort and support our minds: nothing before us but a speedy appearance before the judgment seat of an almighty, infinitely holy, and angry God, and an endless eternity in suffering his wrath without mercy! The person we have been speaking of, had a great sense of this. He said, not long before his death, "It is sweet to me to think of eternity: the endlessness of it makes it sweet. But, oh, what shall I say to the eternity of the wicked! I cannot mention it, nor think of it! — The thought is too dreadful!" At another time, speaking of a heart devoted to God and his glory, he said, "O of what importance is it to have such a frame of mind, such a heart as this, when we come to die! It is this now that gives me peace."

How much is there, in particular, in the things that have been observed of this eminent minister of Christ, to excite us, who are called to the same great work of the gospel ministry, to earnest care and endeavors, that we may be in like manner faithful in our work, that we may be filled with the same spirit, animated with the like pure and fervent flame of love to God, and the like earnest concern to advance the kingdom and glory of our Lord and Master and the prosperity of Zion! How amiable did these principles render this servant of Christ in his life, and how blessed in his end! The time will soon come, when we also must leave our earthly tabernacles, and go to our Lord that sent us to labor in his harvest, to render an account of ourselves to him. O how does it concern us so to run as not uncertainly, so to fight, not as those that beat the air! And should not what we have heard excite us to depend on God for his help and assistance in our great work, and to be much in seeking the influences of his Spirit, and success in our labors, by fasting and prayer, in which the person spoken of was abundant? This practice he earnestly recommended on his deathbed, from his own experience of its great benefits, to some candidates for the ministry that stood by his bedside. He was often speaking of the great need ministers have of much of the Spirit of Christ in their work, and how little good they are like to do without it, and how, "when ministers were under the special influences of the Spirit of God, it assisted them to come at the consciences of men, and (as he expressed it) as it were to handle them with hands: whereas, without the Spirit of God, said he, whatever reason and oratory we make use of, we do but make use of stumps, instead of hands.

Oh that the things that were seen and heard in this extraordinary person, his holiness, heavenliness, labor, and self-denial in life, his so remarkably devoting himself and his all, in heart and practice, to the glory of God, and the wonderful frame of mind manifested in so steadfast a manner under the expectation of death, and the pains and agonies that brought it on, may excite in us all, both ministers and people, a due sense of the greatness of the work we have to do in the world, the excellency and amiability of thorough religion in experience and practice, and the blessedness of the end of such a life, and the infinite value of their eternal reward, when absent from the body and present with the Lord; and effectually stir us up to endeavors, that in the way of such a holy life, we may at least come to so blessed an end. — *Amen.*

The Last Enemy

LAURA MENDENHALL

When a baby girl in her congregation died nine days before Easter, after a very brief and painful life, Laura Mendenhall responded in a personal but also theological way. This is an Easter sermon for the times when "life is not all bunnies and flowers."

As an example of the preacher's craft, this sermon shows how theologically potent a sermon that tells one story can be. Through a narrative of this child's last day of life as she experienced it, Dr. Mendenhall is able to deal worthily with life's uncertainty and tragedy, as well as with baptism, resurrection, prayer, and the hopeful intention to believe in spite of everything.

Dr. Mendenhall preached this sermon on Easter Sunday, 1998, at Westminster Presbyterian Church, Austin, Texas, where she was pastor at the time. Today she is President of Columbia Theological Seminary in Decatur, Georgia.

The Last Enemy

ISAIAH 65; 1 CORINTHIANS 15

I will rejoice in Jerusalem,
and delight in my people;
no more shall the sound of weeping be heard in it,
or the cry of distress.
No more shall there be in it
an infant that lives but a few days,
or an old person who does not live out a lifetime. . . .
They shall not labor in vain,
or bear children for calamity. . . .

ISAIAH 65:19-23

For as all die in Adam, so all will be made alive in Christ. But
each in his own order: Christ the first fruits, then at his com-
ing those who belong to Christ. Then comes the end, when he
hands over the kingdom to God the Father, after he has de-
stroyed every ruler and every authority and power. For he
must reign until he has put all his enemies under his feet. The
last enemy to be destroyed is death.

1 CORINTHIANS 15:22-26

B aptism on Easter Sunday: for centuries the church held baptisms only on Easter, because the message is so strong. We will baptize today. But this year, I had an early taste of an Easter baptism. I want to tell you about this baptism so that when life is not all bunnies and flowers you will remember that we have an Easter story to tell.

Two weeks ago Friday, I was at home writing a sermon. I received a call about mid morning from a young couple in the church. They were calling from the hospital to tell me that the doctors had just informed them that their ten-day-old daughter would not survive her surgery from the day before. They said the chaplain was getting ready to baptize her. Could I come, *now?* I told them I was on my way, shut off my computer, grabbed my keys, flew out the door, and charged across town to Brackenridge Hospital.

Of course I would come. But what if I didn't get there before she died? Did we really need to baptize this dying child? Should I even consider baptizing a child who would never grow up to know and follow Jesus? On the other hand, baptism is about *God's* faithfulness, and if I did not baptize this child, what right did I have to baptize *any* child, or anyone of any age, as far as that goes? A myriad of questions beat upon me as I raced through the parking garage to get to this family. When I arrived, God led me through an Easter baptism.

In spite of the incision in her chest, she was still a beautiful seven-and-a-half-pound baby. Through the dozens and dozens of tubes and wires I reached out to her, caressing her foot, her hand, her precious little knee. What I was frantic to tell these young parents was *why* we would baptize their dying baby.

I blurted out to them that we were not baptizing their

daughter in order to introduce her to God. God already knew their child. As the Psalmist prayed,

> It was you, O God, who formed my inward parts;
> you who knit me together in my mother's womb. . . .

God knew this child even before her parents knew her. Her baptism was not to call God's attention to her. God was already in that room, caressing, comforting — not only this little one, but her parents as well. Baptism was not her introduction to God.

Neither was baptism a quick fix. She was going to die, and there would be millions of questions we would never answer.

Why did this baby have a heart condition in the first place?

Why did the surgery not work for her when it did for others?

Why was one so dearly loved and long awaited not going to make it?

We didn't know. What we did know was that in life and in death we belong to God. In life and in death this child belonged to God. God did not need her to be baptized in order to know or love her, but her baptism would mark her as Christ's own forever.

Having gotten that little sermon out of my system, I was ready to baptize this baby. The chaplain handed me the water and seemed eager to get out of my way. I handed the water to the baby's grandmother, an elder in the Presbyterian Church (U.S.A.). Then, without thinking, I began: "Do you renounce evil and its power in the world?" I could not believe I asked them this question! I wished I could take back any words about evil. On the other hand, this is not a question about their *denying* evil, something they could not do. Rather, this question asked them to *renounce* evil's *power* over them. Still, I chose not to push them for an answer. I went on and asked them if they could turn to Jesus Christ, trusting in his grace and love? I realized that at this point asking them to trust God was also asking a lot of them. But I saw their heads nodding as I fumbled my way into the baptism prayer:

> thanking God for the gift of water which sustains us;
>> praying for God to sustain us even now
>>> through our tears;
> remembering how at the beginning of the world
>> God moved over the watery chaos and
>> called forth life and order;
>> praying God would move over our chaos and
>> call forth life for us;
> remembering how God did not forsake Noah
>> when the flood overtook him;
>> praying God would remember us in our crisis;
> remembering how God parted the waters for
>> the Hebrew people;
>> praying God would part the waters for us
>> because we were drowning;
> remembering how at Jesus' baptism God claimed
>> Jesus as his own Son;
>> praying God would claim this child as God's own.

I prayed that as this child was buried with Christ in her baptism, so she would be raised to new life with Christ in his resurrection.

We baptized her in the name of the Father who had

loved her even before her birth, in the name of the Son whose death and resurrection were for her, in the name of the Holy Spirit who would continue to intercede on her behalf. And in that simple act of baptism we marked her as Christ's own forever.

As I took the water from the grandmother, my hand was shaking and I spilled the water all over my dress. Did I receive part of this baptism? Probably, I hope. The transformation of baptism often spills over on those who are present. I set down what was left of the water and turned around to see that the young mother had found a chair. A nurse asked her if she was okay. She looked up calmly and answered, "Yes, I am. I am not afraid anymore." Did the water of baptism also fall on her?

As we are buried with Christ in baptism, we become dead to an old way of living, dead to life ruled by fear, dead to that which separates us from God. In baptism, even death cannot separate us from God. For in baptism we are united with Christ in his resurrection, raised with Christ to a new life, a life in which we trust God not to forsake us but to raise us up, so that we can live even in the face of death. Resurrection is for those on both sides of the tomb. In baptism, this young mother who was being confronted with death was also being confronted with resurrection.

Now it happened that day that we received a sign that God was hearing our prayers. Be assured, I am not saying that we need to have signs in order to trust God's care for us. If we always had signs, there would be no need for faith. Most of the time, we pray simply in the faith that God hears us and will not desert us. But later that afternoon, we prayed again, and we know that prayer was answered.

I had left the hospital around lunchtime to get back to the sermon, returning to them later in the afternoon. As soon as I walked back into the room, it was apparent that the baby was declining. After checking with the grieving and exhausted family, I took a turn keeping vigil at the crib, rubbing the child's little hands and feet, watching the monitors. As time passed, I realized I was going to have to leave to get to the church for a wedding rehearsal. I asked if we could pray again before I left. As the family gathered at the crib of this dying infant, my heart went out to them, and I dared to ask their permission to pray that Jesus would take their child home. They solemnly nodded.

While I was praying, I was aware that the nurses had entered the room again. When we looked up from the prayer, the nurses were attending the monitors above the crib. Everything had flat-lined. Jesus had answered our prayer, and this little one's baptism was now complete.

We do not always get signs of answered prayer. You know that. But that day baptism became our sign that in life and in death we belong to God. At Easter, the empty tomb became our sign that in life and in death we belong to God. It is in an Easter baptism that we begin to understand how both our life and our death are linked to Jesus' victory over the last enemy to be destroyed, death. Through Christ's profound sign of grace we have been given new life, life in the face of death. Consequently, we are also called to new life, a life where love and justice and mercy abound:

> Where there shall no more be the sound of weeping
> or the cry of distress.
> Where there shall not be an infant that lives

but a few days,
    or an old person who does not live out
      a lifetime. . . .
Where those who build houses shall inhabit them;
    those who plant vineyards shall eat their fruit. . . .
Where we shall not labor in vain,
    or bear children for calamity. . . .
Where the wolf and the lamb shall feed together. . . .
    And no one shall hurt or destroy.

For the last enemy has been destroyed. Thanks be to God.

Standing at the Grave

JEFFREY J. NEWLIN

Jeffrey J. Newlin's sermon is different from the others in this collection, in that it is occasioned specifically by the celebration of the festival of All Saints rather than by the death of a particular child. Newlin makes use of sermons by Friedrich Schleiermacher, William Sloane Coffin, and John Claypool to approach a Christian understanding of grief as a reality of human experience.[1]

---

1. The sermon by Schleiermacher from which Newlin quotes appears in this volume, beginning on p. 145. Coffin's begins on p. 53 above. A different sermon by John Claypool begins on p. 33 above.

Standing at the Grave

1 JOHN 3:1-3

See what love the Father has given us, that we should be called children of God; and that is what we are. The reason the world does not know us is that it did not know him. Beloved, we are God's children now; what we will be has not yet been revealed. What we do know is this: when he is revealed, we will be like him, for we will see him as he is. And all who have this hope in him purify themselves, just as he is pure.

1 JOHN 3:1-3

Today we celebrate the festival of All Saints, when we give thanks for the generations of Christians who have gone on before us, without whose witness we wouldn't have the faith that we have. Appropriately, we've given God special thanks for the members of this church who have died within the last year. Many family and friends of these members are with us today, and for those of you that I'm referring to, the rest of us want you to know that our hearts continue to break for you on account of your grief and sadness. No one ever completely recovers from the death of someone he or she loved; nevertheless, with time can come healing.

But if time can bring healing from grief, even more assuredly it will bring more to grieve about. In the end, death will take us all, and everyone that we love. So this day is not only for the benefit of those who grieve, that they might find solace, but for the benefit of the rest of us as well, that we might be better prepared to grieve when our time comes.

One of the great strengths of the church in the Middle Ages was the training it gave its members in what it called the "art of dying." True, people back then had much more opportunity to learn about death than we have now. Death was a constant companion. Many children died at an early age. Plagues, disease, and war were prevalent. But though the inevitability of death doesn't hang over us the way it hung over them, we are just as much in need of the church's ministry in the art of dying as they were, that our lives too might be deep and mature, not shallow and forgetful. Just as much as our medieval predecessors, all of us need to take regular stock of what life looks like standing at the grave.

What I would like to do with you this morning is study death from the experience of three exceptionally articulate Christians: Friedrich Schleiermacher, an early-nineteenth-century German Reformed theologian, who is generally considered to be one of the greatest theologians in the history of the church, and whose special achievement was to articulate the Christian faith under the challenge of the rise of modern science and biblical criticism; William Sloane Coffin, former chaplain of Yale University, former pastor of Riverside Church, New York, and a renowned social activist; and John Claypool, a well-known preacher today who was a Southern Baptist and is now an Episcopalian.

All three of these men have much to teach us about death, for they all wrote sermons on the occasion of what is surely the most painful acquaintance with death of all: the death of a son or daughter. Schleiermacher's son, Nathaniel, died as a schoolboy of disease. Coffin's son, Alexander, died at the age of twenty-four when, under the influence of alcohol, he was unable to prevent his car from spinning off the road into Boston harbor. Claypool's daughter, Laura Lue, died at the age of ten of leukemia.

When death strikes, some people work through the death by not speaking. Others work through their grief by speaking, and as you read the sermons that I am referring to, the first thing that strikes you is that, quite apart from their intended benefits for the congregations they were delivered to, they are clearly efforts by the preachers to work though, make sense of, somehow ease the pain of their grief. The pain and anguish is so heavy in all of them that you almost wipe the tears off the text.

In his sermon, Schleiermacher said, "Many a heavy cloud has passed over my life; yet what has come from without, faith has surmounted, and what from within, love has recompensed. But now, this one blow, the first of its kind, has shaken my life to its roots."

All three men were shaken to their roots. They were struggling with the kind of pain that radically changes everyone it touches. Would they emerge with any hope, with any joy, with any purpose? They didn't know. So they looked desperately for comfort. Just as desperately, many of their friends tried to give comfort to them. In the process many roads were proposed that offered nothing but disappointment. Significantly, all three sermons begin with the preachers identifying these roads that got them nowhere.

First there is the dead-end road that goes like this: Don't weep. Children who are taken away young are in fact delivered from all of the dangers and temptations of this life and are rescued early into heaven. This consolation is often further expanded by images of all the blessings of heaven that its inhabitants enjoy. How can one be sad for a child when one knows of all the happiness he or she is having before God?

This road brought no consolation to Schleiermacher. Fully admitting that this world is not heaven, he nevertheless knew it to be very good. This life is glorified through Christ and hallowed through the Holy Spirit, Schleiermacher said. He had found great blessings for himself in this life through his Christian upbringing and Christian community. How could he not expect his son to have the same blessings? He found no comfort in his son's days being cut short in this life that he might arrive sooner in heaven.

As for the wonderful images of heaven that are supposed to compensate for this loss, Schleiermacher said that these only raised more questions for him than they answered, and thereby lost much of their power to console.

The second dead-end road considered in these sermons refers to the will of God. It proposes that we must accept whatever happens as the will of God and resign ourselves to it. Claypool said that although there is indeed ancient and practical wisdom in this approach, it is the wisdom of Stoicism, not Christianity. Christianity teaches that God is more than power; God is love. It is not Christian to resign ourselves to fate; what is Christian is to yield ourselves to love.

Not nearly as restrained and philosophical as Claypool, Coffin exploded when this consolation was offered to him. When he heard a middle-aged woman who had brought "about eighteen quiches" to his house say, "I just don't understand the will of God," he instantly was in hot pursuit, swarming all over her: "I'll say you don't understand the will of God," Coffin blasted her, admitting in his sermon that he expressed this anger as much with the hope that it would do him good as with the intention of teaching her something.

Rather than finding consolation in thinking that Alex's death was the will of God, Coffin said, "My own consolation lies in knowing that it was *not* the will of God that Alex die; that when the waves closed over the sinking car, God's heart was the first of all our hearts to break."

Resigning themselves to God's will brought no comfort to either Claypool or Coffin, because its abstract, impersonal approach to God robbed them of what they most needed: the personal presence of God.

The third dead-end road in the sermons is a rush toward tidy answers and easy consolation, especially by quoting Scripture. Claypool said, "I believe that someday God will be able to give account for what he has done and show how it all fits together, but that eschaton is not now." He had experienced too much pain to be satisfied with any simple answers now. How can someone be satisfied with easy answers when he has watched his ten-year-old daughter bite on a rag to distract herself from the pain, and heard her beg him to pray to God to take that awful pain away?

"Have you prayed to God?" Laura Lue asked him. "Yes, I have," Claypool responded. "When did he say it would go away? When did he say it would go away?" Laura Lue's question kept haunting him, and he had to admit to himself that God had said nothing.

When one experiences such pain there are no simple solutions. If there is a simple solution, it can only be despair — the kind of despair Claypool stared straight in the face when he asked himself whether "all of our talk about love and purpose and a fatherly God were not simply a veil of fantasy that we pathetic humans have projected against the void."

And just as Coffin exploded at the quiche-carrying woman who muttered something about the will of God, he also couldn't reject this consolation of easy solutions without calling down judgment on those who offered it — in this case a few fellow reverends who quoted Scripture to him with the hope that his pain would all go away. They knew a lot more about Scripture than about the human condition, Coffin said. They were using Scripture to protect themselves from the bleakness they couldn't face.

"While the words of the Bible are true," Coffin said in his sermon, "grief renders them unreal. The reality of grief is the absence of God — 'My God, my God, why hast thou forsaken me?' The reality of grief is the solitude of pain, the feeling that your heart's in pieces, your mind's a blank, that, in the words of Lord Byron, 'there is no joy the world can give like that it takes away.'"

So all three preachers began their sermons by naming death for the fierce adversary it is, and rejecting simplistic theology and unconsoling consolations. But, significantly, none of the preachers ended his sermon this way. This is, after all, what makes their words sermons. Each of them found before the end some resolution, some hope, and some strength. They found it not in answers to their questions (which they never expected to find), but in a new confidence that through their suffering they had indeed been in contact with God.

Their word to us is very much like Dr. Carlyle Marney's word to Claypool when, just before Laura Lue died, he told him that although he had no word for the suffering of the innocent and never had had, nevertheless, "I fall back on the idea that our God has a lot to give an account for." In other words, without in any way giving up their stubborn insistence that some day God will have to give an account of himself, they just as stubbornly refused to give up their stubborn belief that there was a God with whom they were in contact, who one day would be in a position to give an account of himself to them.

Significantly, all three came to this awareness of God's presence amid their pain through words of Scripture. Schleiermacher said that his comfort and hope came alone in the word of Scripture, modest and yet so rich: "It doth not yet appear what we shall be, but we know that when he appears we shall be like him, for we shall see him as he is," and in the powerful prayer of the Lord, "Father, I would that where I am, they also may be whom Thou hast given me."

Claypool found consolation in the story of God giving back Isaac to Abraham after first requiring his sacrifice. And Coffin, the one who most bitterly complained about the hollow comfort of Scripture rolling off the lips of some of his insensitive clerical friends, concluded by quoting so much Scripture that there is not time for me to quote it all to you now.

It's also significant that all three preachers concluded their sermons with thanksgiving to God. Paraphrasing Job,

Schleiermacher said, "the Lord has given him; the name of the Lord be praised, that he gave him to me; that he granted to this child a life, which, even though short, was yet glad and bright and warmed by the loving breath of his grace."

Coffin gave thanks for his "day-brightener" of a son. And the central point of Claypool's whole sermon was his belief that gratitude for what we have been given, instead of remorse over what we have been denied, is the only way to walk back down from the mountain of loss.

In addition to the resolution that all three preachers found in God's comfort through Scripture and their gratitude for the blessings God has given, Coffin went on to find additional comfort in the wisdom that he was gaining through the painful ordeal. "It's a fact," he said, "few of us are naturally profound; we have to be forced down." And then he quoted lines from Robert Browning Hamilton that he found "trite but true":

> I walked a mile with Pleasure,
>   She chattered all the way;
> But left me none the wiser
>   For all she had to say.
>
> I walked a mile with Sorrow
>   And ne'er a word said she;
> But oh, the things I learned from her
>   When sorrow walked with me.

Can you believe it? Judging by the angry way Coffin treated the woman with the eighteen quiches, and the clergy friends with their words of Scripture, if someone had

had the gall to quote that old chestnut to him, you would think he would have driven him or her through the wall! Yet there he was, quoting the verse himself, and finding comfort in its wisdom.

It's striking, isn't it? All three sermons began by criticizing simplistic faith, yet they found resolution in what, if recommended to others, might itself be taken as simplistic. The difference, of course, is all the grief and struggle that happened in between. That's what keeps all of these sermons from being simplistic, and makes them instead moving and profound.

The way we resolve our grief is a process. Timing is everything. What is inappropriate at one time is a lifeline at another. At the beginning, it is necessary for the one who has suffered loss to admit the pain and to feel it deeply. No one can ever resolve grief without doing this. To deny that the experience of death is the experience of the absence of God is a pious lie that disqualifies anything else one might say.

But once one admits the reality of the emptiness and despair and meaninglessness of death, one is also ready to admit that there is something else present in the darkness as well, something that at first seems only a hint of light on the horizon, but in time becomes a warm glow bathing everything: There is also love; there are also happy memories and gratitude; there is also God. A simplistic life based on despair is no more adequate to the human condition than a simplistic life based on rose-colored theology. In the end, only contact with the living God satisfies.

That is why we need each other so much — not only those fellow believers who are living, but the whole communion of saints who constantly surround us. When our pain is so deep and real that we can't see or feel anything else, we need the witness of the saints about us; saints who, on the basis of their own experience of life's pain, can assure us that though our pain is true, it is not the ultimate truth. In all our pain, and beyond all our pain, always is the beauty, truth, and love of God in Jesus Christ, which never dies, and which will never allow us to die.

Anne Elizabeth Kuzee

JACK ROEDA

Anne Kuzee died of cancer when she was thirteen.

Jack Roeda, her pastor, responded first by acknowledging the abyss of despair and unbelief that could surround the moment. Like biblical lament, he does not soften despair with sentimentality, but also does not let despair be the final word. The sermon ends by refocusing the congregation on Christ and his resurrection, offering an example in Anne's own faith.

Jack Roeda is pastor of the Church of the Servant in Grand Rapids, Michigan, a congregation of the Christian Reformed Church.

Anne Elizabeth Kuzee

JOHN 11:17-27

Martha said to Jesus, "Lord, if you had been here, my brother would not have died. But even now I know that God will give you whatever you ask of him." Jesus said to her, "Your brother will rise again." Martha said to him, "I know that he will rise again in the resurrection on the last day." Jesus said to her, "I am the resurrection and the life. Those who believe in me, even though they die, will live."

JOHN 11:21-25

Dear family and friends of Anne Kuzee,

It was not for lack of love that Anne died. She was deeply loved, and she dearly loved family and friends, and creatures large and small, especially horses.

Nor was it for lack of will that Anne died. She was full of determination, upbeat, spunky. "I will beat this cancer," she said.

Nor was it for lack of medical treatment. For eight years Anne was in and out of the best hospitals. She was cared for by excellent doctors and wonderful nurses.

Nor was it for lack of prayers. Anne prayed, her family prayed. She joined her sister, Lisa, in California for a prayer and healing service. I remember one Sunday our chapel was full of people on their knees, praying for Anne. It was not for lack of prayers that Anne died.

We brought all we had to the table, we brought the best we had, and it was not enough. Anne has died, and our hearts are broken, our throats constricted. We want to cry, scream our loss, our frustration, our rage.

This past week in the newspaper a priest in Belgium, at a funeral service for two small children, is reported to have said, "Is our Lord deaf?" We are shocked to hear the question said out loud, "Is our Lord deaf?" But we know that question. We ourselves wonder, "Does God even care? Can we ever again live and pray confidently?"

There are people, perhaps some of you, who say that death, and especially the death of someone so young and promising, shows that we can never be truly confident again. Life's great sadnesses convict them that we are not the beloved children of any Heavenly Father. They would say that it is best we accept that we are castaways, adrift in a vast ocean of space. There is no Father's strong hand here, no safe harbor.

We are acquainted with such despair: even now we are afraid that it may enter and take possession of our souls. But we do not agree, and we have gathered here, in large part, to help one another to resist the darkness, to listen for God. We want to encourage each other to listen for him in the songs and in the prayers and in the Gospel readings. We have come here in the hope that where two or three are gathered in Jesus' name, there he will be. As a deer pants for water, so our souls pant to know that Christ is present and stronger than death.

We know death is strong. Who would deny it? It has taken Anne from us. It can steal from us nearly everything that is dear and precious. But for all death's fearsome strength, the Christian faith says, it is not the strongest. Jesus Christ is. The drawing on the cover of the funeral liturgy, of Jesus and a child holding hands, was drawn by Anne's sister, Julie. And Anne would say, if she could speak to us, Jesus holds my hand, and don't be afraid, he won't let me go.

In John's Gospel, Jesus makes a staggering claim: "I am the resurrection and the life" (11:25). It tells us that the resurrection is no mere doctrine or holy possibility. Jesus himself is the embodied presence of that resurrection life. "I am the resurrection." Jesus is God's life to a dying world. In him death has been defeated, and to be sheltered in him is to have here and now the life that is eternal. Jesus asked Martha, "Do you believe this?" Martha said she did. So did Anne.

Dr. Diane Komp, a pediatric cancer specialist who teaches at the Yale University School of Medicine, became a believer in Jesus through the testimonies of children she treated for cancer. In one of her books, she writes, "A few years ago a close friend struggled with widespread cancer. On a drive to Boston following a chemotherapy cycle, we made many emergency stops. . . . One time, she got back in the car, looked up at me with a mischievous little-child grin to say, 'This is going to sound very corny. The big C is not cancer: the big C is Christ.'"[1]

---

1. Diane Komp, *A Child Shall Lead Them* (Grand Rapids: Zondervan, 1993), p. 107.

An ancient Easter hymn makes a similar declaration:

Sin's bonds severed, we're delivered;
Christ has crushed the serpent's head.
Death no longer is the stronger;
Hell itself is captive led.
Christ has risen from death's prison;
O'er the tomb he light has shed.

The big C is Christ.

Before we moved to our present facilities, we worshipped in a school gym. In between the two morning services, I would sometimes sit in a large closet off the gym floor to collect my thoughts. While I was sitting there one Sunday morning, some children of the church began playing a game of tag outside my door. Anyone tagged was out of the game, but, as I heard the rules, if you had your hand on the closet doorknob, you were safe. So as I sat there, more or less in the dark, I heard the children running and shouting and playing their game. And now and again I would hear one of them shout, "No, you can't tag me. I had my hand on the knob. I'm safe; I'm not out." Now years later at this funeral service, sitting more or less in the dark, we tell ourselves, Anne has her hand on Jesus. Listen . . . we can hear her: "I'm safe. Suffering and death cannot touch me here. I'm not out. I'm safe."

We and Anne belong — body and soul, in life and in death — to our faithful Savior Jesus Christ. It is our only comfort.

Reaching Out

FLEMING RUTLEDGE

When death takes the young, it always raises questions of faith. What, if anything, was God doing in this situation?

In response, Fleming Rutledge does not resort to propositions or to logic. There are philosophical ways to address the questions, and these can be helpful. But here she acknowledges the painful reality that Mark Freeman, who died of AIDS as a young man, reached out for God at the end of his life, but saw no clear sign that God had responded.

Then she does what she knows Christians have always done in the face of death: she tells the story of Good Friday and Easter. It is a hard answer, not an easy one, and therefore it is an answer worthy of the questions.

At the time of Mark's death, Fleming Rutledge was on the staff of Grace Episcopal Church in New York City. "Mark Freeman" is a pseudonym.

Reaching Out

For if we have been united with Christ in a death like his, we shall certainly be united to him in a resurrection like his.

ROMANS 6:5

In the last year of his life, Mark Freeman reached out for God.

This may sound like very hollow news to those of you who loved him. Humanly speaking, there is no evidence that God responded. For many of you who have suffered one loss after another, there must be many questions: Is there a God at all? Does he care? If he cares, why doesn't he do something?

I remember vividly the day that Martha Sherwood brought me to meet Mark at Grace Church. We were standing in the aisle after the service, and she introduced me to him, and it seemed to me then and there that we should pray. There were two teenagers standing by, whom I knew well, so I invited them into the circle, and there we stood,

Mark, Martha, two teenagers completely new to the situation, and me, with our arms encircling each other, and we prayed aloud and for a long time. We prayed that he would be healed and we prayed that he would be defended.

I have often thought since about that prayer. Was it heard? Was there any response? Where is there any evidence that prayer to God makes any difference?

Shortly after, Mark joined a prayer group at Grace Church, which he attended for about two months until his activities were curtailed by illness. The members of that prayer group are here tonight. One of those members told me that Mark had prayed with great authenticity and honesty during those two months, perhaps more so in some ways than anyone else. What of those prayers? Where did they go? Were they of any use? Does any of it make any sense, or was it all just a last desperate attempt to bargain with death? Is there anybody to hear prayer? And if so, who? And if God, why doesn't he *do* something?

I have been grappling with these questions for a very long time in my own life. I am not, as it happens, one of those that has a lot of victorious prayer stories to tell. In fact, the husband of a dear friend of mine who was very ill for many years used to say gloomily, "Every time we pray, she gets worse." To me, there seems to be a lot of unanswered prayer out there; I suppose it's partly a matter of whether or not you see the glass as being half full or half empty, but even Jesus said, "There were many lepers in Israel at the time of the prophet Elisha, and none of them was cleansed but one, Naaman the Syrian" (Luke 4:27). Jesus healed many people, but there were far more whom he did not heal, for his own inscrutable reasons. Experiences in my own family have led me to the conclusion that we are simply not able to fathom the mystery of random suffering.

Some people smoke and drink and shoot up and waste their substance in riotous living and survive to be eighty, while others live quietly and conservatively and make significant contributions to society and are snuffed out in the prime of their lives. People who are wildly promiscuous are alive and a faithfully monogamous couple is dead. It makes no sense. Where could God possibly be in all this? Mark Freeman, described by his friends as being fiercely devoted to the quest for truth, would not have stood for any glib answers at his funeral, and I am not going to give any.

What I am going to do is what Christians have always done from the beginning. I am going to return to the story. Mark, like all writers of fiction and drama, was a storyteller, and at its heart Christianity is a story. Contrary to popular opinion, it is not, in the final analysis, a story about humanity reaching out for God; it is a story about God reaching out for humanity. It is a story about God grasping us before we even knew anything was happening. In fact, so serious was our failure to recognize God when he came among us that we crucified him. God came down into our world in human flesh, in an authentic bodily existence, to share our frailty and weakness, to live under the sign of death as we do; and we crucified him. It was the ultimate proof that "the good die young."

When I am talking with a person who is suffering irrationally and asking the deep questions, this is the part of the story that I usually focus on — the death of Jesus, his human destiny, his oneness with us in our fragility, in our pain, in the extremity of our need. Often, people find this to be the most compelling part of the story.

But when I was talking with Mark about this, he said something very interesting and unusual; in his intense, thoughtful way, he said, "I never have been much attracted to the suffering Christ." He spoke about the way that the cross was stressed in his evangelical upbringing, and said that the crucifixion somehow did not speak to him at the deep level where his pain was.

This is the Easter season, part of what the church calls the Great Fifty Days, beginning on Easter Sunday and lasting through Pentecost. On this third Wednesday of Easter, 1988, I would like to tell you another piece of the story.

I thought about Mark's remark for days afterward. You can imagine that it took the wind out of my sails somewhat; I had brought out the heavy artillery and it had misfired. What else was there to say?

A few days later I received what I thought seemed to be an answer. I wish I could tell you that it was the occasion for a great breakthrough for Mark. I can't tell you that, because when I next visited him he was really too sick to respond very much. Nevertheless, I am convinced that it is the right message for us tonight as we ask the hard questions and grope in the dark for some reassurance, some hope.

The Christian story does not end with the crucifixion. The end of the story is not an end at all, but a commencement of the most unthinkable proportions. I sat down and wrote Mark a letter, a letter that perhaps — I see this now — had as its ultimate destination this gathering tonight, in this Easter season. I wrote something like this: "Mark, forget about the crucifixion for now. Focus on something else. Focus on the resurrection of Jesus Christ from the grave. That's your message."

This is the way the story goes. Jesus was dead. He was as dead as anyone has ever been dead; not technically dead for a few minutes only to be resuscitated by heroic medical procedures, but thoroughly, certifiably, irreversibly dead — and they buried him. In a grave. With an enormous stone over the entrance.

And then he was alive. The tomb could not hold him. The stone was simply blown aside by God's returning life — not returning *human* life, which always ends in dissolution and death, but *God's* life, which is triumphant over anything and everything that threatens human existence, including most of all dissolution and death. The resurrection of Jesus Christ means that God has reversed the story, reversed the odds, reversed the direction — from death to life.

Later on, you will be hearing readings from Mark's own writings. One of his friends told me that he believes, now, looking back from this perspective, that there was faith there all along, even though Mark had not been to church for many years. God, you see, was reaching out for him all along. Even before Mark knew it, even before he could identify it, God had reached out for him. I don't mean that God reached out to take him away from us — nothing so superficial, glib, and unsatisfying as that. No, I mean that God reached out for him the way God reaches out for us all — to make us his own. St. Paul writes, "For if we have been united with Christ in a death like his, we shall certainly be united to him in a resurrection like his" (Romans 6:5).

I do not know if Mark was convinced of this or not. But even if he was not, even if he couldn't see it or feel it, even if you can't see it or feel it — even if I can't — nevertheless, *this story is true*. This is what the Easter season means. Jesus Christ has been raised from the dead. It's true. And *as in Adam all die, even so in Christ shall all be made alive* (1 Corinthians 15:22). Amen.

Sermon at Nathanael's Grave

FRIEDRICH SCHLEIERMACHER

In histories of Christian thought, Friedrich Schleiermacher is often placed at the beginning of a new era. He opened the path of nineteenth-century Protestant theology, first in his native Germany and later for the Protestant world, by identifying faith with a sense or feeling of absolute dependence. Introspection became the basic theological task. As a theologian, Schleiermacher was never content with the received answers; he had to examine the whole of Christian faith anew.

When his son Nathanael died, Schleiermacher found that he had to explore that situation anew as well. The usual consolations did not help him. Consolation was not what Schleiermacher wanted. Instead, he speaks in uncontained grief of his hope in God, his gratitude for Nathanael's life, and his desire that parents and teachers cherish the children in their care.

Schleiermacher (1768-1834) was a minister of the Prussian Union Church, after playing a key role in its founding. For much of his career he was professor of theology at the University of Berlin.

Sermon at Nathanael's Grave

JOHN 17:20-26

Father, I would that where I am, they also may be whom Thou hast given me.

JOHN 17:24

My dear friends, come here to grieve with this stooped father at the grave of his beloved child, I know you are not come with the intention of seeing a reed shaken by the wind (Matthew 11:7). But what you find is in truth only an old stalk, which yet does not break even from this gust of wind that has suddenly struck him from on high, out of the blue. Thus it is! For a happy household, cared for and spared by Heaven for twenty years, I have God to thank; for a much longer pursuit of my vocation, accompanied by undeserved blessings; for a great abundance of joys and sorrows, which, in my calling and as a sympathetic friend, I have lived through with others. Many a heavy cloud has passed over my life; yet what has come from without, faith has surmounted, and what from within, love has recompensed.

But now, this one blow, the first of its kind, has shaken my life to its roots.

Ah, children are not only dear pledges entrusted to us from God, for whom we must give account; not only inexhaustible subjects of concern and duty, of love and prayer: they are also an immediate blessing upon the house; they give easily as much as they receive; they freshen life and gladden the heart. Just such a blessing was this boy for our house. As the Redeemer said that the angels of the little ones see the face of his Father in heaven (Matthew 18:10), so with this child it appeared to us as if such an angel beamed out from his countenance the kindness of our God. When God gave him to me, my first prayer was that fatherly love would never mislead me to expect more of the boy than was right; and I believe the Lord has granted me this. I know very well that there are children far more outstanding in gifts of mind, in eager alertness, and upon whom far greater expectations concerning what they will accomplish in the world could be raised, and I would rejoice should there be many of them. When I gave him the name he bore, not only did I want thereby to greet him as a precious and welcome gift of God; I wanted at the same time to express my earnest wish that he might become like his biblical namesake, a soul in which there was no falsehood; and this too the Lord has granted me. Honest and frank as our boy was, he looked everyone in the eye full of trust, doing only good to all, and we have never found anything false in him. And for this reason, my dear children whom I see around me here — because he was truthful — he also remained free from many sorrows which otherwise come even upon those of your age. A selfish nature was also something far from him, and he bore love and goodwill for all humanity. So he lived among us as the joy of the whole house. And when the time was come that it seemed necessary to transplant him to a larger community of young people and a wider circle of education, there too he began to acclimate himself and to thrive, and even the deserved and well-meant reprimands of his teachers fell on good soil.

Thus I had thought to follow him with fatherly eye still further, and I quietly waited to see to what degree his intellectual powers would further develop and to which area of human activity his inclination would turn. If I often said to myself — though in a sense wholly other than that which has now come to pass — that it would not be granted me to complete his upbringing, I was nonetheless of good courage. I regarded it as one more beautiful blessing of my calling that, in days to come, he would never fail to find faithful fatherly advice and strong support upon my account, though I hoped he would not fail to find it on his own account as well.

This charge, important above all others for the remainder of my life, to which my heart clung full of love, is now ineradicably stricken through; the friendly, refreshing picture of life is suddenly destroyed; and all the hopes which rested upon him lie here and shall be buried with this coffin! What should I say?

There is one consolation, with which many faithful Christians soothe themselves in such a case, which already many beloved, friendly voices here have spoken to me in these days, and which is not to be simply dismissed, for it grows out of a correct assessment of human weakness. Namely, it is the consolation that children who are taken away young are in fact delivered from all of the dangers and temptations of this life and are early rescued into the sure Haven. And this boy would certainly not have been spared these dangers. But, in fact, this consolation does not want to take with me, I being the way I am. Regarding this world as I always do, as a world which is glorified through the life of the Redeemer and hallowed through the efficacy of his Spirit to an unending development of all that is good and godly; wishing, as I always have, to be nothing but a servant of this divine Word in a joyful spirit and sense; why then should I not have believed that the blessings of the Christian community would be confirmed in my child as well, and that through Christian upbringing, an imperishable seed would have been planted in him? Why should I not have hoped in the merciful preservation of God for him also, even if he stumbled? Why should I not have trusted securely that nothing would be able to tear him out of the hand of the Lord and Savior to whom he was dedicated, and whom he had already begun to love with his childlike heart — for one of his last rational responses in the days of his sickness was a warm affirmation to the question of his mother, whether he loved his Savior rightly. And this love, even if it was not fully developed, even if it had undergone fluctuations in him: why should I not indeed have believed that it would never be extinguished for him, that it someday would have possessed him wholly? And as I would have had the courage to live through all this with him — to admonish him, to comfort, to lead — therefore this way of thinking is not as consoling to me as it is to many others.

Still others who grieve generate their consolation in another way, out of an abundance of attractive images in which they represent the everlasting community of those who have gone on before and those who as yet remain behind; and the more these images fill the soul, the more all the pains connected with death are stilled. But for the man who is too greatly accustomed to the rigors and cutting edges of thinking, these images leave behind a thousand unanswered questions and thereby lose much, much of their consoling power.

Thus I stand here, then, with my comfort and my hope alone in the Word of Scripture, modest and yet so rich, "It doth not yet appear what we shall be, but we know that when he appears we shall be like him, for we shall see him as he is" (1 John 3:2), and in the powerful prayer of the Lord: "Father, I would that where I am, they also may be whom Thou hast given me" (John 17:24). Supported by these strong beliefs, then, and borne along by a childlike submission, I say from my heart, the Lord has given him: the name of the Lord be praised (Job 1:21), that he gave him to me; that he granted to this child a life, which, even though short, was yet glad and bright and warmed by the loving breath of his grace; that he has so truly watched over and guided him that now with his cherished remembrance nothing bitter is mixed. On the contrary, we must acknowledge that we have been richly blessed through this beloved child. The Lord has taken him: his name be praised, that although he has taken him, yet he has left us, and that this child remains with us here also in inextinguishable memories, a dear and imperishable individual.

Ah, I cannot part from the remains of this dear little form, ordained for decay, without now, after I have praised the Lord, expressing the most moving thanks of my heart:

before all, to the dear half of my life through whom God gave me the gift of this child, for all the motherly love and trust which she bestowed on him from his first breath to his last, expired in her faithful arms; and to all my beloved older children, for the love with which they were devoted to this youngest and which made it easier for him to go his way, bright and happy, in the straight path of order and obedience; and to all the beloved friends who have rejoiced in him with us, and with us have cared for him; but especially to you, dear teachers, who made it your pleasure to take an active part in the development of his soul: and to you, dear playmates and schoolmates, who were devoted to him in childlike friendship, to whom he was indebted for so many of his happier hours, and who also mourn for him, since you would have liked to go forward with him still farther on the common way. And to all of those who have made this hour of parting more beautiful and celebrative for me, my thanks.

But with thanks it is always good that some gift be joined in return; and so, all of you, accept as a remembrance of this moment, so painfully significant for me, a well-meant gift of Christian admonition. My wife and I have both loved this child tenderly and with all our hearts, and what is more, amiability and gentleness are the ruling tone of our household. And yet, here and there, there steals through our memories of our life with this beloved child a soft tone of reproach. And so I believe that perhaps no one passes on, concerning whom those who lived most closely with him are completely satisfied when they examine themselves before God — even if the allotment of life has been as short as this one. Therefore let us all truly love one another as persons who could soon — alas, how soon! — be snatched away. I say this to you children; and you may believe that this advice, if you follow it, will tarnish no innocent joys for you; rather it will surely protect you from many errors, even though they may be small. I say this to you parents; for even if you do not share my experience, you will enjoy even more unspoiled the fruits of this word. I say it with my sincerest thanks to you teachers; for even if you have to do with young people in numbers too great to allow you to develop a special relation with each individual, yet all the more must those things which you do to keep order and good discipline be infused with the right spirit of holy Christian love. Ah yes, let us all love one another as persons who could soon be separated!

Now, thou God who art love, let me not only resign myself to thy omnipotence, not only submit to thy impenetrable wisdom, but also know thy fatherly love! Make even this grievous trial a new blessing for me in my vocation! For me and all of mine let this communal pain become wherever possible a new bond of still more intimate love, and let it issue in a new apprehension of thy Spirit in all my household! Grant that even this grave hour may become a blessing for all who are gathered here. Let us all more and more mature to that wisdom which, looking beyond the void, sees and loves only the eternal in all things earthly and perishable, and in all thy decrees finds thy peace as well, and eternal life, to which through faith we are delivered out of death. Amen.

Where the Children Can Dance

PHILIP TURNER

Pregnancy brings hope, at least in the best situations. Parents who are ready to welcome children into their lives can now focus their hope on one individual. They begin indirectly to know and love that one with growing anticipation. Occasionally, though, the fallenness of creation intrudes.

Brendan Turner lived and died the focus of such love and anticipation. He was delivered after his death, with spina bifida, a cleft palate, and club feet. His parents named him, while seeing that there was no reason to baptize him.

His mother writes, "Neither of us had ever been to a funeral for an unborn child, and we weren't sure if it was something that was done, but we both agreed that it was the right thing to do. . . . Philip wrote the following meditation and read it during the service. It was what we believe to be true of Brendan's life, what we saw to be true of Christ's body, and what we believe to be true of our life in God."

Philip Turner is a former dean of the Berkeley Divinity School at Yale.

Where the Children Can Dance

ISAIAH 11:6

. . . and a little child shall lead them.

ISAIAH 11:6

Brendan Joseph Albert Turner lived for seven months.
He never saw the light of day. From the beginning he
was terribly wounded, and in the end his wounds proved
too much for him. He died as he lived, quiet and unseen,
cuddled in his mother's womb. When he was born, his parents held him, wept, called him by name, and said goodbye;
but from now on they will know him only by his absence.

We cannot know much about Brendan's life and death,
what is graced and what is a sign of the terrible wound from
which we all suffer. Any quickly spoken word, even a word
of comfort, is bound to be false. For a clear vision of the
meaning of his life and our own we shall have to wait until
the great day on which the truth of all our lives is made
known. Then and only then will we know, even as we are
known.

For the time being we can see only in part, but by faith we can see enough to give us hope. If we know how to look, we can see extraordinary things in the midst of this horror. Brendan's birth was an occasion for discerning the body of Christ. His mother and father have been carried in the arms of the church like little children. They have been cared for as people would care for a wounded part of their own body. They have been taken by the hand, protected, and given freedom to weep and be afraid.

Sometimes on this earth we are blessed with a glimpse of people who adore God and who love those others God has given into their hands as they love themselves. Sometimes on this earth we catch a glimpse of what the life everlasting is like; Brendan's death was such an occasion.

Brendan's death has also shown us the most important thing we can know about ourselves. His body was wounded and his life short. He was cheated both of life's pain and of its pleasure. It is true that his life might have been one of unendurable pain, but we cannot say that with certainty. He might also have known joys far greater than any possible for us who are reckoned to be "normal."

We cannot weight the pluses and minuses of his life, but we can see ourselves in him. We can see that one day we will be as helpless and wounded as he was from the day of his conception. We can see that our lives, like his, are short, and that their transfiguration is as dependent upon the grace and power of God as is his. In the end there are none of us who are not Brendan, and if we will look we may see that we are held to the breast of God as he is.

And if we by faith look into the heart of this horror, we will see the nature of greatness. The greatest of us is the least and the least the greatest, because greatness is given only to those who know that they live by grace alone. The fathomless love of God is all that Brendan has. We delude ourselves if we believe we have more.

It is Brendan and millions like him who will lead us all into the kingdom of heaven. That great company which no one can number will be led by the little ones. By grace, the night before they discovered that Brendan was dead, a friend asked his mother and father if they had an image of Jesus that they held before them as guide and comfort. Both said no, but what they said then is not true now. They do have an image of Jesus, and it is this: There is a company of children dancing and singing, and Jesus walks behind them like a good shepherd. Because they are so protected, they can skip freely and without care before the throne of God.

Surprised by Death

James Van Tholen

Cornelius Plantinga called attention in *Christianity Today* to James Van Tholen's courageous sermon confronting his own impending death. Introducing the sermon, Plantinga wrote,

> In 1996 James Van Tholen, then 31, and his wife, Rachel, moved to Rochester, New York, where Jim became pastor of a Christian Reformed Church. Members of the church found themselves drawn to Jim's ministry, especially to his preaching, which gleamed with biblical intelligence and humane understanding.
>
> Then, the unthinkable occurred: in the late winter of 1998, physicians identified and surgically removed a liposarcoma from behind Jim's right knee. Within weeks Jim had another tumor behind his chest wall, and then spots on both femurs and one kidney. Recent tests confirm cancer up and down Jim's spine, with the result that he now thinks about how he moves, always conscious of the risk of spinal cord compression (and paralysis).
>
> From March until October, Jim struggled to recover from surgery and to absorb forms of chemotherapy that offered no cure but could prolong his life somewhat. By October, the chemother-

apy had suppressed Jim's cancer enough that he was able to return to his pulpit.

What follows is the sermon Jim preached from Romans 5:1-11 on the morning of his return, October 18, 1998. As the members of the congregation listened to their young preacher's sermon, they understood something about dying and rising with Christ that they hadn't known just that way before.[1]

James Van Tholen died January 22, 2001.

1. Cornelius Plantinga, "Surprised by Death: A Young Pastor Discovers What Grace Looks Like While Battling Cancer," *Christianity Today* 43, no. 6 (May 24, 1999), p. 57.

Surprised by Death

For while we were still weak, at the right time Christ died for the ungodly. Indeed, rarely will anyone die for a righteous person — though perhaps for a good person someone might actually dare to die. But God proves his love for us in that while we were still sinners Christ died for us. . . . For if while we were enemies, we were reconciled to God through the death of his Son, much more surely, having been reconciled, will we be saved by his life.

ROMANS 5:6-10

This is a strange day — for all of us. Most of you know that today marks my return to this pulpit after seven months of dealing with an aggressive and deadly form of cancer. Now, with the cancer vacationing for a little while, I am back. And of course I'm glad to be back. But I can't help feeling how strange this day is — especially because I want to ignore my absence, and I want to pretend everybody has forgotten the reason for it.

But we can't do that. We can't ignore what has happened. We can rise above it; we can live through it; but we can't ignore it. If we ignore the threat of death as too terrible to talk about, then the threat wins. Then we are overwhelmed by it, and our faith doesn't apply to it. And if that happens, we lose hope.

We want to worship God in this church, and for our worship to be real, it doesn't have to be fun, and it doesn't have to be guilt-ridden. But it does have to be honest, and it does have to hope in God. We have to be honest about a world of violence and pain, a world that scorns faith and smashes hope and rebuts love. We have to be honest about the world, and honest about the difficulties of faith within it. And then we still have to hope in God.

So let me start with the honesty. The truth is that for seven months I have been scared. Not of the cancer, not really. Not even of death. Dying is another matter — how long it will take and how it will go. Dying scares me. But when I say that I have been scared, I don't mean that my thoughts have centered on dying. My real fear has centered somewhere else. Strange as it may sound, I have been scared of meeting God.

How could this be so? How could I have believed in the God of grace and still have dreaded to meet him? Why did I stand in this pulpit and preach grace to you over and over, and then, when I myself needed the grace so much, why did I discover fear where the grace should have been?

I think I know the answer now. As the wonderful preacher John Timmer has taught me over the years, the answer is that grace is a scandal. Grace is hard to believe. Grace goes against the grain. The gospel of grace says that there is nothing I can *do* to get right with God, but that God has made himself right with me through Jesus' bloody death. And that is a scandalous thing to believe.

God comes to us before we go to him. John Timmer used to say that this is God's habit. God came to Abraham when there was nothing to come to, just an old man at a dead end. But that's God for you. That's the way God likes to work. He comes to old men and to infants, to sinners and to losers. That's grace, and a sermon without it is no sermon at all.

So I've tried to preach grace, to fill my sermons up with grace, to persuade you to believe in grace. And it's wonderful work to have — that is, to stand here and preach grace to people. I got into this pulpit and talked about war and homosexuality and divorce. I talked about death before I knew what death really was. And I tried to bring the gospel of grace to these areas when I preached. I said that God goes to people in trouble, that God receives people in trouble, that God is a God who gets into trouble because of his grace. I said what our Heidelberg Catechism says: that our only comfort in life and in death is that we are not our own but belong to our faithful Savior, Jesus Christ.

I said all those things, and I meant them. But that was before I faced death myself. So now I have a silly thing to admit: I don't think I ever realized the shocking and radical nature of God's grace — even as I preached it. And the reason I didn't get it where grace is concerned, I think, is that I assumed I still had about forty years left. Forty years to unlearn my bad habits. Forty years to let my sins thin down and blow away. Forty years to be good to animals and pick up my neighbors' mail for them when they went on vacation.

But that's not how it's going to go. Now I have months, not years. And now I have to meet my creator who is also my judge — I have to meet God not later, but sooner. I haven't enough time to undo my wrongs, not enough time to straighten out what's crooked, not enough time to clean up my life.

And that's what has scared me.

So now, for the first time, I have to preach grace and know what I'm talking about. I have to preach grace and not only believe it, but rest on it, depend on it, stake my life on it. And as I faced the need to do this, I remembered one of the simplest, most powerful statements in the entire Bible.

You may have thought that the reason for my choice of Romans 5 lay in the wonderful words about how suffering produces endurance, and endurance produces character, and character produces hope. Those are beautiful words, true words, but I'm not so sure they apply to me. I'm not sure I've suffered so much or so faithfully to claim that my hope has arisen through the medium of good character. No, many of you know far more about good character than I do, and more about suffering, too.

It wasn't that beautiful chain with character as the main link that drew my attention to Romans 5; instead, it was just one little word in verses 6 and 8. It's the Greek word *eti*, and it has brought comfort to my soul. The word means "yet" or "still," and it makes all the difference between sin and grace. Paul writes that "while we were *still* weak Christ died for the ungodly." He wants us to marvel at the Christ of the gospel, who comes to us in our weakness and in our need. Making sure we get the point, Paul uses the word twice in verse 6 in a repetitious and ungrammatical piling up of his meaning:

"*Still* while we were *still* weak, at the right time Christ died for the ungodly."

I'm physically weak, but that's not my main weakness, my most debilitating weakness. What the last half-year has proved to me is that my weakness is more of the soul than of the body. This is what I've come to understand as I have dwelled on one question: How will I explain myself to my God? How can I ever claim to have been what he called me to be?

And, of course, the scary truth is that I can't. That's the kind of weakness Paul is talking about. And that's where *eti* comes in — while we were *still* weak, while we were *still* sinners, while we were *still* enemies of God, we were reconciled with him through the death of his Son. I find it unfathomable that God's love propelled him to reach into our world with such scandalous grace, such a way out, such hope. No doubt God has done it, because there's no hope anywhere else. I know. I've been looking. And I have come to see that the hope of the world lies only inside the cradle of God's grace.

This truth has come home to me as I've been thinking what it will mean to die. The same friends I enjoy now will get together a year, and three years, and twenty years from now, and I will not be there, not even in the conversation. Life will go on. In this church you will call a new minister with new gifts and a new future, and eventually I'll fade from your mind and memory. I understand. The same thing has happened to my own memories of others. When I was saying something like this a few months ago to a friend of mine, he reminded me of those poignant words of Psalm 103:15-16: "As for mortals, their days are like grass; they flourish like a flower of the field; for the wind passes over it,

and it is gone, and its place knows it no more." For the first
time I felt those words in my gut; I understood that my place
would know me no more.

In his poem "Adjusting to the Light," Miller Williams ex-
plores the sense of awkwardness among Lazarus' friends
and neighbors just after Jesus has resuscitated him. Four
days after his death, Lazarus returns to the land of the living
and finds that people have moved on from him. Now they
have to scramble to fit him back in:

Lazarus, listen, we have things to tell you.
We killed the sheep you meant to take to market.
We couldn't keep the old dog, either.
He minded you. The rest of us he barked at.
Rebecca, who cried two days, has given her hand
to the sandalmaker's son. Please understand
we didn't know that Jesus could do this.
We're glad you're back. But give us time to think.
Imagine our surprise. . . .
                          We want to say
we're sorry for all of that. And one thing more.
We threw away the lyre. But listen, we'll pay
whatever the sheep was worth. The dog, too.
And put your room the way it was before.[1]

Miller Williams has it just right. After only a few days,
Lazarus' place knew him no more. Before cancer, I liked Wil-

1. Reprinted from *Adjusting to the Light: Poems* by Miller Williams, by permission of the University of Missouri Press. Copyright © 1992 by Miller Williams.

liams's poem, but now I'm living it. Believe me: hope doesn't lie in our legacy; it doesn't lie in our longevity; it doesn't lie in our personality or our career or our politics or our children or, heaven knows, our goodness. Hope lies in *eti*.

So please don't be surprised when in the days ahead I don't talk about my cancer very often. I've told a part of my story today, because it seemed right to do it on the first day back after seven months. But what we must talk about here is not me. I cannot be our focus, because the center of my story — *our* story — is that the grace of Jesus Christ carries us beyond every cancer, every divorce, every sin, every trouble that comes to us. The Christian gospel is the story of Jesus, and that's the story I'm called to tell.

I'm dying. Maybe it will take longer instead of shorter; maybe I'll preach for several months, and maybe for a bit more. But I am dying. I know it, and I hate it, and I'm still frightened by it. But there is hope, unwavering hope. I have hope not in something I've done, some purity I've maintained, or some sermon I've written. I hope in God — the God who reaches out for an enemy, saves a sinner, dies for the weak.

That's the gospel, and I can stake my life on it. I must. And so must you.